Paperback ISBN 9781780922003
ePub ISBN '9781780922010
PDF ISBN 9781780922027

Published in the UK by MX Publishing
335 Princess Park Manor, Royal Drive, London, N11 3GX

www.mxpublishing.co.uk

Cover design by
www.staunch.com

Dedicated to Pippa

Contents

Values and beliefs have started wars, genocides and put man on the moon - match the employer's values and beliefs and become unstoppable

- **Rule No.8 Make Your Interview Passionate**   *page 27*
A passionate speech can influence thousands of people, mobilising a new workforce or persuading individuals to take arms against their oppressors. Be passionate and believe in your argument, influence the employer with passionate expression

The Expert Interview: Influential Rules 9 to 14

- **Rule No.9 MI5 Agent Technique**   *page 31*
MI5 agents use rapport, influence and manipulation to infiltrate the enemy; they become an expert in the disguise and character identity, convincing the enemy that they are someone they are not

- **Rule No.10 Cheat the Interview**   *page 33*
Never lie obviously, give generalised feedback to questions and let the interviewer make their own opinion. Say your answers with confidence and quote researched information like it is your own opinion, as long as it highlights your expertise

- **Rule No.11 Learn the Secret Language of Interviews**
     page 36
A secret language is used in sector specific interviews, learn this hidden communication and appropriately utilise terminology. With just a few memorised sentences verbalised in this foreign tongue you can appear fluent in this strange language

- **Rule No.12 Secret Detective**   *page 37*
To solve the case you need to dissect the crime scene and research the suspects, identifying key details in the investigation. In the interview knowledge is power; your research will help you locate the winning interview formula

- **Rule No.13 Undersell Yourself at Your Peril**   *page 38*
Dry and dull interviews will not do you any favours, make the conversation light, fun and intriguing, using this opportunity to

highlight all your relevant transferable skills — you must make yourself sound like a well rounded package

- **Rule No.14 Wear a Condom** *page 43*
Stay safe! Being caught in a tricky situation can break or make the interview, seduce the employer by playing it safe until they are under your control, once manipulated you can lead and direct the interview

Commanding Confidence: Influential Rules 15 to 23

- **Rule No.15 Not Cocky But Confident** *page 48*
Act how you want to be seen, make this impression last and in time you will naturally adopt this character unconsciously

- **Rule No.16 Pain and Pleasure** *page 49*
Choices and decisions are made through the motivational influence of pain and pleasure (the carrot and stick) by controlling your own pain and pleasure influences you can delete interview fears and access interview confidence

- **Rule No.17 Limit the Limiting Beliefs** *page 52*
A person's belief system will change the direction of their life from failure to success, in an interview your belief system alone will be the difference to a job offer or an interview failure

- **Rule No.18 Steal Confidence From Others** *page 57*
Can you really be accused of thievery when you're only stealing mental information and systems from others? This technique will open new doors for you, just don't get caught doing it!

- **Rule No.19 Give Your Voice a Boost** *page 63*
Have you ever attended a meeting when all you wanted to do was fall asleep as the speakers/chair/your co-workers were so boring — their voices monotone droning on. Entertain your interviewer with your voice

- **Rule No.20 Show Your Nerves, Confidently** *page 66*
Too much confidence means you're too cocky, but if you're too nervous then you're no use to any employer. Win job interviews

with a mix of confidence and nervousness; learn when you should sound nervous and when you should project confidence

Negative self talk will kill your interview, don't listen to the devil in your head or it will be the death of you, eradicate negative self talk and feel a new growth in confidence

Our subconscious mind teaches us how to act in situations through learning from our past experiences. But when these experiences are negative your subconscious will attempt to keep you away from similar experiences, to overcome the fear of interviews you need to destroy any attached negative memories

A person can have a real fear of spiders, heights and even job interviews as with all phobias these can be overcome but this often takes years of therapy. NLP offers us a way to rid your phobia quickly

Sneaky Interviews Tricks: Influential Rules 24 to 29

Anxiousness controls you and will destroy your spirit, keeping you awake the night before the interview. An instant sleep technique will relax you, calm you down and offer you the best chance on the day of the interview

You are trying to impress people with your appearance, communication skills and body language, don't let your moist hands let you down; this simple technique will change the interviewer's first impression of you

The interviewer is always trying to figure out the real you, a neutral handshake won't give too much away which will intrigue

The 73 Rules of

Influencing the
Interview

Using Psychology, NLP and
Hypnotic Persuasion Techniques

By Chris Delaney
Employment King
www.employmentking.co.uk
www.christopher-delaney.com

the employer, but an overpowering handshake shows dominance - which is best for you?

A feeble voice portrays weakness, answer interview questions with power and confidence; find your God voice

Impress the interviewer with your memory capacity. Increase your power of influence by being able to recall an abundance of information, facts and figures

Your body speaks volumes; with a little training you can use your posture to gain acceptance, to build rapport and to illustrate authority

Mind Read the Employer: Influential Rules 30 to34

Why wait for the employer to speak before you start to influence the interviewer, a master influencer will be able to read the non verbal cues giving them the edge over other applicants and dominate the interviewer

Without knowing it the interviewer will give away their feelings and thoughts through their body language, use this silent communication to control the interviewer

The eyes are the windows to the interviewer's soul, hidden in them are the clues as to what we are thinking, go one step further and use the eyes to mind read the interviewer giving you a real advantage over other less committed interviewees

Words have power; the language you use can give you an edge, creating instant rapport and likeability or creating disinterest and confusion, leading to a breakdown in communication and likability

- **Rule No.34 Build Likeability through Commonality** *page 97*
People like people who are like them, to influence your interviewer focus on commonality and build on this growing friendship as we find it hard to say no to someone we like

Persuasion through Personality: Influential Rules 35 to39

- **Rule No.35 Energise the Interviewer** *page 100*
The difference between Extrovert or Introvert interviewers is how they acquire their energy, by mastering how to influence this personality trait you will increase the spirit of the interview

- **Rule No.36 Influence the Interviewers Decision Making Process** *page 101*
The interviewer's role is to make a decision - to choose the best candidate. By influencing the interviewer's decision-making process you can, at the extreme persuade the interviewer to employ you

- **Rule No.37 Disguise the Information You Give the Employer** *page 103*
We process information differently depending on our personality type, once you master how your interviewer will filter your information you can use this knowledge to infiltrate the employer's thought process

- **Rule No.38 Deliver Your Answers the Way They Will Be Best Understood** *page 104*
Interview stress kills the interview, the interviewer after interviewing all day will feel pressured, tired and on the edge of annoyance – be sure not to fall into the trap of stressing the interviewer by wrongly presenting the structure of your interview

- **Rule No.39 Persuade Through Personality** *page 106*
We are all different which means to be successful in all interviews you need to change your approach to influence each

individual interviewer. A one way approach will be the death of your interview persuasion technique

Interview Questions and Presentations: Influential Rules 40 to 47

a real interview as a rehearsal, testing your manipulation with your true purpose concealed

Part Two – The Interview

Interview Arrival: Influential Rules 48 to 51

Understand the interviewer's requirements and use this as bait, offer the interviewer what they want, add a little extra and they will be hooked

Rapport – The Key to Success: Influential Rules 52 to 56

- **Rule No.52 Gain the Interviewers Agreement**   *page 137*
Nodding at the interviewers key points will increase rapport, once in rapport you can encourage agreement by nodding while explaining your key selling points which will influence the interviewer to agree with you

- **Rule No.53 Infect the Interview**   *page 137*
Likeability and rapport will affect the interview outcome, once you learn how to increase rapport you will affect the interviewers view of you at the bare minimum with an increase of likeness and at the utmost creating a passionate connection

- **Rule No.54 Take the Interviewer on a Journey of Discovery**
page 140
Be the author of the interview, take control by pacing the interviewer and use rapport to direct and lead the interviewer on a new journey

- **Rule No.55 Interrogate the Competition**   *page 142*
Everyone has a weakness, a fault, their own Achilles heel; it may be insecurity, procrastination or even an obsessive compulsive disorder, discover the limitations of the competition and exploit this

- **Rule No.56 Create an Aura of Power**   *page 145*
A group interview is one way for the employer to quickly disqualify those that they feel are lacking in the essential criteria required for the position. To stand out in a group interview you need to create an aura of power while making the other interviewees seem weak and helpless

Persuasive and Hypnotic Language Patterns: Influential Rules 57 to 67

Mess with the interviewer's mind, use reverse psychology - suggest that they don't offer you a job which will compel them to offer you the position, the interviewer won't understand why they are so compelled to hire you

- **Rule No.64 Conceal Your Intentions by Simulating Choice**

Suggest choice but don't offer any, the interviewer will believe they have options but in reality they will have none

- **Rule No.65 Make the Puppet Dance**

Control the interviewer, put your words in their mouth and make them think and act the way you want them to, at the bare minimum you will lead the employer, when used with proficiency you will be in command

- **Rule No.66 Use Social Proof to Influence – get others to highlight your strengths**

People are sheep who will follow others and believe what they are told without any proof, sway the interviewer by quoting your past employer's high appreciation of you

- **Rule No.67 Create a Fantasy**

Hidden meanings are understood unconsciously through stories and metaphors; create intrigue, anticipation and the interviewer will want to know more, this technique can help create a strong identity

Winning Job Interviews: Influential Rules 68 to 73

- **Rule No.68 An Argument Will Only Show Your Weakness**

Negative putdowns can rupture the whole interview process and will make you look weak; handling negativity masterfully will not only save your skin but put the power back in your hands

- **Rule No.69 Turn Around the Tide of Power; Interview the Interviewer**

The power in an interview is unbalanced, take control, switch around the balance of power and gain authority - be careful this technique can back fire if you over exert your new found power

The Author

Chris Delaney is a Hypnotherapist, Careers Advisor and NLP Life Coach and the founder of Employment King.

He prides himself on supporting people to achieve all their life and career goals using a mixture of therapy that best suits the individual client.

You like millions of other people have bought this book, (or at the very least have deemed it interesting enough to pick up in a book shop) as you're reading this introduction, you are feeling intrigued about how you can learn to influence the interview process using NLP, psychology and hypnotic persuasion techniques. **This book does come with a warning;** my mission is to help people like you secure more job offers, so many that you are able to take your pick from the endless list of employers who have been influenced to offer you a position, which means **you will be learning some dark and secretive persuasion techniques.**

Job hunters have never had it so hard, the recession has made it easy for the employer's to have the power, this book will teach you the dark side of interview manipulation, giving you the power back. With fewer jobs around and competition at an all time high, you don't just need to stand out at the interview - you need to influence the interviewer.

This book is unlike other interview books, many of these old style interview guides fail to add value to interviewee performance, describing tired techniques and advising the reader to do common sense things that most people would already do. There is little value to be drawn from a text that drones on about getting a good night's sleep or answering questions with confidence, they are telling us what we must do but not <u>what we actually need to do and how to do it!</u>

This is why we have gone above and beyond all other interview books, as **you will learn the secrets of influencing and persuading the job interview**, these techniques can be dark and dangerous especially if you use the technique to <u>turn other interviewees into nervous wrecks,</u> but I would add these techniques will get you ahead of the game and as a result you will win more job offers.

I need at this point to reiterate that this book comes with a <u>WARNING</u>, the powerful techniques you are about to uncover are used successfully by **master influencers, successful pick-up artists, powerful business leaders and notorious con artists.**

You are probably already thinking about the hundreds of ways you can use hypnotic persuasion techniques during the job interview, so now we will look further. The techniques you are about to learn work as our mind is powerful but can be easily influenced – try this next exercise:

Read the Text Below Aloud.

I
Love
London In The
The Summer Time

Were you one of the 99 out of a hundred people who fell for this little mind trick? Did you read the word THE twice? Read it it again! It says I Love London in **The The** Summer Time, did you spot the double use of the word IT as well?

This may be a simple mind trick but it is the process in this trick that we can use in job interviews to increase your job offers. We have uncovered the psychology of interviews and you will shortly be learning how to manipulate the employers' unconscious, making them want to recruit you. We have taken **the best from NLP, Psychology and Hypnotic Persuasion** and broken it down to make it relevant to the job interview. The techniques are easy to learn, by following the step by step instructions ensuring you will perform at your very best at every job interview.

The book is a guide with **73 influential rules** that you must follow to influence the interview; you can read the book from cover to cover or dip in and out of the sections that are most relevant to you, from the rules designed to give you **Instant Confidence** to rules that will teach you how to con the employer, so they believe your an **Industry Expert**. Others may desire to delve deeper, drawing on the techniques in the **Dark Side of Sales Psychology** and **Hypnotic Language Pattern** sections.

If you're still in the book shop, reading this book you will want to buy it now as you will want to practice these powerful influencing techniques before your next job interview, because **the recession has put a demand on all jobs, with over 300 candidates applying for each individual position!** In addition as an extra bonus you can download our best selling interview question and answer e-book **Tricky Questions Killer Answers – over 60 interview questions and answers** for FREE, with this purchase.

We have crammed in so much expert knowledge that we want to share with you; you might ask why am I giving away so much information in one book? It is true that I could have created two books with this material and increased my profits, but my mission isn't to have two bestselling books, my mission is to <u>help you achieve the career success that you **deserve.**</u> I have met thousands of job hunters just like you, who like you are talented, experienced and unemployed or stagnating in a job because they are scared of rejection or don't yet know the **73 rules of interview influence.**

Do you really want to stay in a job you hate? Do you want to be turned down from even more job applications? Do you like to feel like a failure? A reject? No, you don't and you don't deserve to. **This book will change your future**; imagine you could pass any job interview, while feeling confident and persuasive – **The 73 Rules of Persuasion** will give you a short cut to interview success, giving you the edge over other applicants by destroying the competition, while manipulating the interviewer.

Finally I want to offer you the best of luck with your next job interview, let me know your interview success stories, e-mailing to:

<u>info@employmentking.co.uk</u>

Part One
Preparing for Success

Sales - The Dark Side of Psychology:

Influential Rules 1 to 8

As a young job hunter, I had been invited to an interview for a sales job; I was relatively disinterested in the role but desperate for a job. I was mortified to be asked within the first five minutes to have to **Sell** a pencil to the interview panel. My opening was terrible;

"Erm... do you want to buy this pencil?....It's really good...erm...you can write things down and then erase them if you don't like what you wrote.... it only costs about..5p"

At the time I was probably impressed with my performance, it could have been a lot worse, being quite shy and hating being put on the spot I wasn't what you might deem a natural salesman. To hear **"Is that it?"** was a real slap in the face, my prospective employer proceeded to take the pencil from me to take the opportunity to show me how it should be done.

"You there!" he boomed with confidence, pointing a finger directly at me.

"Do you know how many uses this pencil has?"

"No" Came the shaky reply, unsure if this was still a job interview.

"If you owned this amazing Z10 pencil, name three things you would use it for?"

"Erm...writing shopping lists, homework and..I suppose drawing"

"So you want a Z10 pencil that can be used to build lists, create technical drawings and a pencil that will help answer tricky exam questions?"

"Yes..I think-"

"Given a choice would you want to buy a pencil that can create sketches, write lists and can be used to complete all of your homework with ease OR would you buy a pencil that can do all these tasks plus more?.." I was sold.

"...A pencil that can write under water and in outer space, a pencil that can erase mistakes with a flick of the hand using the Z10 Eraser designed by NASA scientists – NOW which would you choose?"

"The last one, sir" – the dynamic had switched to teacher- pupil by this point as he dominated the conversation.

"Now, how much would you pay for this pencil?"

"Erm..well..around..."

"How much is it worth, a pencil that can write in outer space, designed by NASA scientists?" he pressured.

"A pound?" I shouted.

His raised eyebrows signalled that I had given the wrong answer.

"No I mean two pounds."

"So, you want to pay 2 pounds for this pencil, don't you?" It was agreed.

"Well, as I like you and you have shown yourself to be an affable type of chap, you can buy one Z10 pencil for £2 or 2 for £2.50, what will it be?" he asked while reaching over to take a second similar pencil from his desk tidy.

I left that interview with two pencils, no job offer and the foundations of understanding the importance of sales techniques in job interviews.

Let me start by asking you - do you want to win more job offers?

Of course you do, to win more job offers you first have to understand **the power behind sales techniques**, before you skip forward to the exciting chapters on influential language patterns that can be used to bypass the interviewer's conscious mind persuading them to offer you any job, you first need to understand how to sell yourself, as this is a critical part to all job interviews.

Why do people buy certain goods over other products? What influences a persons' unconscious mind, when all they originally wanted was a bottle of milk and 30 minutes later they walk out of the supermarket with a bottle of milk nestled amongst a trolley full of impulse purchases that they didn't initially go in for?

Imagine you understood sales psychology even on a basic level, what if you knew how to turn your skills and experiences into an irresistible product for the employer? You are probably already thinking of hundreds of ways you can use sale techniques in your next job interview, but first ask yourself is a job interview really just a sales pitch?

Rule No.1
Blow Out The Competition With a Secret Sales Pitch

"I don't want to have to sell myself; I want to be natural, if they don't like me it's there loss" <u>DIRECT QUOTE from Thousands of Unemployed people</u>.

The fact is **an interview is in essence a secret sales pitch**, you can be yourself, you can be natural, but you have to sell your skills, qualities, qualifications and experiences.

So many failed job hunters HAVE the skills and experiences required by the employer and in many cases the <u>employer does miss out by not employing them</u>. But during the interview if the interviewee undersells themselves, then the employer has no choice but to recruit the other less talented candidate.

I have met thousands of people just like you who desire a job, who can't pass interviews even though they are the best in their field – remember employers only know what you tell them about yourself during the interview.

So let's get started, to influence the interview you need to first have an end game, **what are the 3 key points you want the employer to remember about you?** What 3 pieces of information will secure you a guaranteed job offer? What do you have (skills, qualities, experiences, qualifications, etc) that the other job hunters don't posses? What are your key selling points? What value will you add to their organisation?

These could include your experience, your attributes, qualities or anything you think the employer would be extremely impressed with.

Record them here, now:

_____
_____
_____

Did you write down your selling points? 5 out 10 people who bought this book didn't, as they continued to read on but I would add, the techniques in this book will help you win more job offers and this will increase with each of the exercises completed, so if you didn't write anything down, go back and do it now.

Throughout the interview you need to answer each interview question, referring to at least one of your unique selling points, showing the employer how **you can add value to their organisation**, forming the employers overall impression of you. By referring to your unique selling point in a variety of ways, you will be secretly selling your skills to the employer without them realising what you are doing. In marketing the rule of 7 states **"a customer needs to see or hear about a product 7 times before they purchase it"**

So with your end game in mind and armed with a list of your most impressive selling points you can use the psychology of sales to sell your key selling points in 3 easy steps, using the techniques used by the masters in the field of sales.....

Rule No.2 Three Steps to Annihilation

"Here is a simple but powerful rule ... always give people more than they expect to get" - Nelson Boswell

The secret to winning job interviews is <u>learning how to sell yourself</u>, this often sounds harder than it really is, as most people have never had to sell anything before (unless your applying for sales positions) Think back to a time when you purchased something, a holiday, a car or even a new coat. Take the holiday - How did you choose the destination, hotel and airline?

To make your choice you had a list of criteria, one person going on holiday will look for a place with sun and sea, somewhere they can relax and chill out – it must have lots of bars and restaurants serving up delicious food.

A second holiday seeker will be looking for somewhere full of excitement, a place where you can go off the beaten track, a place full of activities; rock climbing, hiking and canoeing. They seek adventure not rest.

Once a Holiday Sales Representative has gleaned this information they can match your criteria to the suitable holidays in their range and will be able to sell you the perfect holiday (they will also use some sneaky description/language tricks that you will learn in future chapters). This scenario is the same during job interviews; once you have gleaned this information from the employers you will be able to understand the employer's criteria and match yourself to this and SELL yourself to them.

Don't think too much about interview questions and answers yet, we will come on to that later. First though write a list of criteria the employer requires. If you're struggling use job adverts, job profiles, job specifications or do some research! The employer's criteria often include qualifications, experience, skills and qualities.

Record down your criteria here; remember if you don't understand your customer's criteria you can't sell them anything.

Example Job Criteria	Job Criteria
<ul><li>**5 years experience in X**</li><li>**Negotiation skills**</li><li>**Excellent communication skills**</li><li>**Able to quickly build rapport MBA Qualification**</li></ul>	

Step one: Now you know the employer's criteria, you can answer each interview question using an answer that matches one of the employer's criteria. Often interviewees will make the mistake of talking at length about irrelevant information which can quickly turn the employer off. Imagine you wanted to purchase a family car with a big boot for the pram and shopping bags, etc but the Car Salesperson keeps talking about sports cars and how fast they can go, you would quickly be turned off, wouldn't you?

Step two: You need to sell and highlight your benefits; these can be the benefits or selling points you recorded at the start of this book. When answering interview questions don't just give general information **"I have 10 years experience in X..."** explain how this will add benefit to their organisation, project and team **"I have 10 years experience in X which mean's A, B and C..."** the successful Car Salesman will match the customers criteria to the benefits of the product – in this case the car.

"This is a great family car, I have kids myself and I know how hard it is trying to fit all the daily essentials - bags, prams, shopping and children into a small car. One of the benefits of this model is the big boot size, you can fit in a pram and 5 shopping bags in this boot, it also has 2 free booster seats and specialised seat belts designed to keep children safe during the unlikely event of a car accident, this is new technology only available in this model, let me show you how it works..."

Step three: A salesperson will summarise, reiterating the features that they observed received the most interest from the customer. As an interviewee you need to imbed a clear impression of your key benefits throughout the interview, at the end of your interview answer summarise the criteria you have sold them during each individual interview question:

"To summarise I would say..."
"You will agree having X skill/experience means I can..."
"Overall I would say...."
"You asked me about my ability to X and I have supplied you with a scenario when I effectively displayed this behaviour.."

The three steps to annihilation (and how to sell anything)

1. **Understand the customer's criteria (in this case the customer is the employer)**
2. **Highlight the benefits of the product (<u>you</u> are the product)**
3. **Reinforce the benefits by summarising**

You need a threefold understanding of the employer's essential criteria, an understanding of the psychology of job interviews and to understand how to use the interviewers hard wired programme of comparison to your advantage...

Rule No.3 Stand Next to Stupid and Look Smart

"The better I get, the more I realize how much better I can get"
- Martina Navratilova

One thing you can guarantee during any interview is that the interviewer will quickly stereotype you and compare you to other interviewees; we have all heard that employers make an opinion about you in the first 5-10 minutes of the interview, this is true but the timeframe is closer to 5-10 seconds.

On a basic level we stereotype people to assess in the first seconds of meeting them if they are a danger or not, this is a primeval instinct. As we have evolved our unconscious minds uses fashion (the clothes the person is wearing), posture and accent among many other things to quickly assess a new person to see what "grouping" they belong to.

We all identify with certain groups and feel an association and affinity to some more than others, we are in each in possession of a "Social identity" - This could be based on our nationality, profession, age, hair colour, ethnicity, hobbies, sports team or values. It can be any characteristic, feature or trait that you feel associates you with a particular group of people, creating an "Us" and "Them."

If you can quickly identify a common trait with the employer to one of their particular groups, you will have the opportunity to forge an instant bond. We see this all the time in the workplace, in a large office the formation of groups will occur often based on a common trait. Look at your workplace, how many groups have formed and for what reason?

We quickly put the people we meet into groups; in some cases an interviewer can form an unfavourable opinion of the interviewee due to their perception of the candidate and the group to which the interviewer thinks they are allocated to. All is not lost at this point, when you have identified that this snap judgement has occurred you need to get to work breaking this stereotype early on by giving evidence that contradicts this belief.

Now we will look at this in practice, an employer may stereotype teenagers, believing all teenagers are lazy with no ambition or drive. In order to break this limiting belief a teenager will employ tactics to break the interviewer's stereotype – **"In my last position I was quickly given a promotion, due to the extra responsibilities I undertook..."**

As well as stereotyping you the employer will automatically compare you to the other applicants. So, is this good or bad? – Well it all depends on the other interviewees.

We all make comparisons often without realising it, when out shopping for a bottle of wine as a gift, which bottle of wine would you consider expensive?

A bottle that cost: **£3.99**   **£5.99**   **£7.99**

Research has proven that most people would consider the £7.99 bottle of wine as expensive when compared to the other two bottles of wine, with many people wanting to purchase the £5.99 bottle (the middle of the road price) believing that the £3.99 bottle will be cheap, nasty and taste bad.

But what if there were 4 bottles of wine;

| £3.99 | £5.99 | £7.99 | £9.99 |

Which wine would you purchase as a gift for your loved one now? First, most people would no longer consider the £7.99 bottle as expensive even though the £7.99 bottle is still the same price as in the original scenario and surprisingly more people would purchase the £7.99 bottle once there is a forth more expensive bottle on offer.

This is because we compare everything we see, this is one way our unconscious mind makes sense of the world. So next time you're in a supermarket buy the product at the price you originally went in to spend, as supermarkets understand and invest a large sum of their profits in researching and implementing selling psychology and will place more expensive products next to middle price products to make you purchase the middle price rather than the cheaper one.

Interviewers do the same with interviewees – they compare us, unlike supermarkets though this is often done unconsciously. If the other interviewees perform poorly and your performance is average then the interviewer will see you as a strong applicant. If you perform well and the other interviewees perform exceptionally well, the employer will see you as a poor candidate, through comparison.

This can seem obvious when you read it, but why do so many people fail to win over interviewers? To win interviews, you need to understand that your performance is just one aspect of the interview and how other applicants perform is equally important. Many applicants knowing they have the required experience and skills don't always try as hard during the job interview believing their experience will see them through but this lack of effort can be their downfall as the employer recruits a less experienced but more enthusiastic employee.

A final thought on comparison is that the interviewer won't remember everything that was said and the way you acted throughout the interview, as we all delete, generalise and distort the world we live in, which means you will be compared to an edited version of the other interviewees - but more on that later.

Understanding psychological aspects of the job interview including comparison is important, but to influence the interviewer you first need to understand what your customer requires from you, the product.....

Rule No.4 Get Inside The Interviewer's Head

"Confidence and enthusiasm are the greatest sales producers in any kind of economy" - O. B. Smith

A Salesperson will tell you, if you understand your customer you can sell anything to them. They will also tell you the importance of observing the golden rule that the customer is always right. We all know that the reality is that customers are often wrong, but there is no better way of losing out on a job position than when a difference of opinion during an interview turns into a disagreement, so what this means is that you sometimes have to let things go. Although, if you are finding it difficult at the interview stage to get along with your prospective employer then perhaps they are not the employer for you!

To understand your customer (the interviewer) you have to understand what they are thinking or how they perceive their world. To understand how we all perceive the world differently, complete this quick exercise;

- Think of a mini car and write down what you see in your mind's eye, recording all the details; the colour, the condition, the environment, whether the car is parked or moving?
- Now ask 3 willing candidates to complete the same activity – to think of a mini car and write down what they see, just as you did, recording all the details; the colour, the condition, the environment, whether the car is parked or moving?

I can guarantee that all of your friends will have a different description of a mini even though all were given the exact same instructions.

We all have our own map of the world (we all see things differently) due to our personal filters (filters: your beliefs, your values, how you take in information through your senses; sight, audio, taste, smell and feelings and your current state) people using these filters, will **generalise, distort** and **delete** information to make sense of their world.

Your brain has to process thousands of pieces of information a second and this is why <u>your brain will **generalise, delete** and **distort** information</u>. Imagine trying to cross a busy road and your brain starts concentrate on the sound of a passersby's mobile ringtone, rather than **deleting** this sound to concentrate on crossing the road. Your hands have a weight, but you delete the feeling of the weight in your arms until you choose to think about this and it enters your conscious mind.

To make sense of the world we often **distort** information due to our past experience, you may have come across this in the past when you have been walking down the street and you recognise an old friend only to find when you get closer to the person it's not the old friend you thought it was. Magicians use distortion for tricks, they may show you a playing card from a pack, the **King of Hearts** but the card suit colour will be Black rather than Red – this will **distort** the information you have received, enabling the magician to trick you to think you have seen the King of Spades instead of the King of Hearts.

To make quick decisions our mind will **generalise** information based on our previous experiences. We all generalise, just think of all the times you may have heard people saying positive and negative stereotypes in everyday conversation:

"Women are bad drivers"   *"Blondes are dizzy"*
"Men can't cook"
"Women are better multi-taskers"
"All students are intelligent"
"Italians are the best cooks"
"Male hairdressers are gay"

We **generalise** every day, we have learnt that doors open one way at a young age, so we generalise that all doors open that way, which helps us speed up decisions rather than having to spend conscious time thinking about how to open each particular door that we are faced with.

The aim of the interview apart from receiving a job offer is to communicate your point to the interviewer, but interviewers will often interview all day and will **delete, generalise and distort** what you say, they will even remember the interview differently to how it really happened with some interviewers believing someone else's answers were yours and vice versa.

Due to this unconscious trick of the mind, you need to repeat your key selling point which is the main reason why you have to summarise your interview answers. To make the interviewer not only remember you and your answers (and key selling points) you need to make your answer relevant to them using their language which you will learn how do later in the book.

Never presume the employer will think the way you do, as you have seen in the Mini-exercise people create different images in their mind from the same question. Ensure you build a positive image of yourself by describing a detailed picture of you throughout the interview, it is like reading a character in a book **"A tall attractive women walked through the office"** you have now created an image in your mind, is the women blonde or brunette? Is she wearing a dress or a business suit? The author throughout the initial chapters will add detail to the character **"Her beauty was natural, her manner unpolished and unrefined but when she looked at you it felt like she was staring onto your soul.."**

Has this altered the picture in your mind's eye? Don't leave your answer open to interpretation allowing the interviewer to generalise, delete or distort your interview answers unless their interpretation creates a distorted version of you that actually paints you in a more positive light, in which case leave well alone!

As you use the techniques you are learning in this book, during your job interview the interviewer will be in constant rapport with you and will start to generalise and distort your answers in a positive way, deleting any negative information, as the interviewer will search your answers to focus on your positives.

But be aware if your interview is not going well, as the interviewer will then unconsciously search and focus on your negatives. Your mind is a powerful tool but can only concentrate consciously on a number of tasks at one time by focusing on what you tell your mind to focus on. You may have come across this when you can't find your car keys; you keep telling your mind **"I can't find my car keys."** Your mind than concentrates on not finding your car keys so you can't see the car keys even when there on a table in front of your eyes, until someone comes in and points them out to you.

The trick to winning all your job interviews is to focus the interviewer's mind on your strengths, skills and key qualities, relevant to the position you are applying for. This is achieved through rapport, confidence and influencing techniques. You need to come across as a positive investment, a valuable commodity and you need the interviewer to see <u>Value</u> in you....

Rule No.5 Become a Valuable Asset

"If you are not taking care of your customer, your competitor will" - Bob Hooey

Think back to when we discussed the price of a bottle of wine, out of the 4 bottles of wine which one do you think will taste the best? £3.99, £5.99, £7.99 or £9.99 bottle of wine?

Obviously most people would say the £9.99 bottle, because we all relate cost with quality. You see this all the time, imagine you wanted to treat yourself to a special holiday for a special anniversary and money wasn't a problem, which holiday would you pick?

- Holiday one costing £999.99 for one week
- Holiday two costing £599.99 for one week

Because you're looking for a special holiday, most people will book the more expensive one as **expense = quality** even though we don't have any of the basic holiday information, including the destination.

To get the interviewer to see you as a quality investment you need to highlight your value. So how much are you worth in monetary terms?

£_____

You need to believe that <u>you are worth employing</u>; you need to show your value and your worth, as an interviewer will pick this up unconsciously which is why we added the chapters on confidence building. If you could give yourself a value in monetary terms what would it be? I hope your answer was in the six figure region, if not re-look at yourself, look at your skills, qualities and everything you can bring to an organisation – write these down and ask yourself again **"How much am I worth?"**

Record – What you can bring to an organisation?
•
•
•
•
•
•
•
•

Once you believe your worth, this belief will transfer itself to interviewers who will pick this up during the job interview, because if you act confident they will believe that you are confident. A con artist is able to successfully con people as they act and seemingly believe that what they are doing/acting/selling is legitimate, legal, honest and beneficial to the person they are conning.

Throughout the interview you will be selling your skills, qualities and strengths, with each selling point the employer will see the value in you.

As an example, by discussing your long list of dedicated clients throughout the interview to the interviewer, will lead them to infer that you may have a caseload of clients or business contacts that you will bring to a new organisation, the employer will see this as a great opportunity to increase their profit. Possessing a skill is seen as valuable, imagine your skills and experiences are in turning around underperforming teams, making companies of the brink of closure profitable – **you are indispensable** - no employer in this situation could afford to turn you down – you are a valuable commodity.

Value can put employers off, when applying for a job that is seen below your academic or experience level. The employers may feel you have applied for this role as a "stop-gap" until you find a better paid position. In this case think about how supermarket use sale psychology: **"Was £19.99 Now Only £7.99 – limited time only"** we all love a bargain, which means you can present yourself as a real bargain to the employer, if you are challenged on this particular point you should tell them;

"I agree I could get a higher paid salary with my qualifications and experiences, but my passion is X (company benefit such as "helping vulnerable people" "working in a job sector that does X") which means I can bring my skills and experiences to this organisation, as this is the job role that I intend to turn into a successful career"

One final thought on value, when negotiating your wage after a job offer, you need to first set the value high <u>by you first setting the initial offer</u>, the employer will then come in under what you stated, but due to you setting the mark high (this has to be realistic) you will often receive a higher salary compared to when the employer sets the first initial offer, which is often low.

This is because we use the initial offer as a baseline and then the employer and employee negotiate from this first offer, all the following negotiations or salary offers are compared to the original offer as we naturally compare everything.

In this example the employer's original offer is £25,000, your counter offer is £35,000, the final offer will be around £30,000.

If you set the initial offer for the same position at £42,000, the employer's first offer will be around £30,000 which means the final offer will be around £35,000.

Now obviously these figures and offers will vary depending on your experiences, negotiation skills and the employer's business acumen, but the point is by setting the initial offer high, highlighting your value, you will be offered a higher wage while leaving the employer believing that their shrewdness has secured them a good deal (you asked for £42,000 and accepted £35,000 - £5,000 more than you would have accepted if the employer set the bar low with his initial offer).

As you have stated your perceived value in monetary terms with your initial offer, the employer is forced to offer you a higher salary as they can't offer a salary that is dramatically lower unless they believe that you are not worth the money or if the company has set a non-negotiable salary limit for your position.

Once you can see the value you are worth, the tide of powers will change, use this new power to influence, manipulate and to get your own way...

Rule No.6 Alien Manipulation

"For every sale you miss because you're too enthusiastic, you will miss a hundred because you're not enthusiastic enough" -Zig Ziglar

Let's forget about job interviews for a second and imagine you currently work for the LS Chocs Bar Company as a chocolate bar sales person. And on this day the earth in invaded by an amicable variety of aliens. After the initial shock humans realise that the aliens have only landed at earth to refuel and they are willing to exchange gold bullion for food. Hearing this, your manger sees for the opportunity to increase sales, hoping to monopolise the alien chocolate bar market. You are sent to sell the aliens a million LS Chocs bars.

While at the negotiations, preparing to make the sale of a lifetime what would you say to sell the aliens a million LS Chocs bars? What benefits would you discuss? What words would you use?

Record everything you would say here:

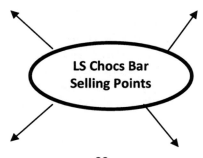

Look back at your mind map, hopefully as you understand the importance of selling on a more conscious level, you would have record a large list of selling points. Previous clients have used:

- **Full of energy**
- **They come in different sizes**
- **A pocket sized treat**
- **Nut free for those with allergies**
- **Full of sugar for instant energy**
- **They taste really nice**

As you can see from your list and the list from my previous clients, <u>all the selling points are positive</u>. There are no negative comments about the chocolate bar rotting your teeth, making you put on weight or causing an onset of acne, as this wouldn't help you help you SELL the product.

It is the same in job interviews; <u>you need to state your positives</u> and ignore the negatives. During job interviews nerves can easily take hold of you, often nervous people waffle to fill silence rather than savouring these opportunities to regroup your thoughts and within these waffles we will often spill out negative information.

"I'm a really good time keeper....100% of the time...unless I have to get the bus if my husband has the car but we all know how public transport can be unreliable, probably about as unreliable as my alarm that didn't go off today... but ...I was really lucky as I rushed to make it just on time, it's great to be here..."

<u>The more you do something the better you become at it</u>; a baby starts by making undistinguishable sounds, very quickly these turn into words. You need to be fully aware of your selling points, the more you think about your skills, qualities and strengths the more easily you will be able to discuss them during the interview, which means you will want to record a list of your skills, strengths, qualities and career successes here. Examples are provided to get you started

– although by now you should be forthcoming with your key selling points!

Skills
- **Typing Speed 40 WPM**
-
-
-

Qualities
- **Ability to mediate and empathise with all people**
-
-
-

Strengths
- **Familiarity and interest with worldwide markets – experience on international scale**
-
-
-

Career Successes
- **Headhunted and subsequently employed by Publicity department within current organisation to interview for new role**
-
-
-

The key to winning more job offers is knowing your key selling points, what you can offer the employer (your value from the employer's perspective) but what really makes you stand out from the interview crowd is passion, by knowing what YOU value in your career will allow you to find your passion and passionate workers make the best employees and all employers know this, so what do you really value?....

Rule No.7 Discovering the Power of Values

"It is not your customer's job to remember you. It is your obligation and responsibility to make sure they don't have the chance to forget you" - Patricia Fripp

What do you value in a career? What is important to you in a job or company? Your values tell you what is right or wrong and how to act, your values make a big difference to you enjoying your career or have that Sunday evening feeling of dread swiftly followed by the Monday morning blues.

Values

What is important to you in your career? Write down your answers below:

Example Values	Your Values
Money Career progression Working with others Seeing the end result to my work Working close to home Having targets Feedback Personal development Flexibility Reliability Ongoing support Variation	

Now you have a list of your career values; you need to reorder them according to importance, which of your values is more important to you? If you had a choice would you take a job that had value A or value B?

Your Values in Order of Importance
1.
2.
3.
4.
5.
6.
7.
8.
9.
10.

Once you know your career values and the values you most require, ask your self **could I have a job that didn't have Value X?** – Pose this question for all the values on your list.

People who accept a job offer with a company who don't have the same values will soon become bored, agitated or stressed, which will lead to them quitting their job or becoming depressed and falling ill. If you have not reflected on and identified your values then you may fall into the trap of applying for similar unsuitable roles in which you quickly become bored, creating a cycle of negative career choices.

Take your top 3 values and ask **"Why is it important to me to have X value?"** as an example; Variation – because I get bored quickly and when I am bored I tend to feel low and have time off work, which often leads to me being sacked. This will help you understand your values in more detail and is an insight to what motivates you - **Pain or Pleasure**? But more on motivational traits later.

Once you know what you truly value in a career, you can match your values to that of the position you are applying for and I would add, once you find your values in the position you are applying for you will quickly become more excited about the position and this excitement will shine through during the interview which will lead to leaving a lasting positive impression. Often enthusiastic, passionate and motivated interviewees gain job offers over experienced but boring interviewees – candidates might give the same answers but they are not always heard the same by the bored interviewer.

Your values drive who you are, for a successful career pick <u>a role and a company</u> that have the same values that you require to thrive - what you believe is important to you. By knowing your values you can now find your hidden passion....

Rule No.8 Make Your Interview Passionate

"You are surrounded by simple, obvious solutions that can dramatically increase your income, power, influence and success. The problem is, you just don't see them"
- Jay Abraham

One thing that will really get you noticed and remembered during a job interview is your passion. When coaching clients meet me for a session, they react positively to my passion for helping people, which means they know that they will get a good service. My clients are right of course, as I put my all into helping other people become successful. This passion motivates me to constantly update my knowledge and improve my skills, I constantly read coaching/self improvement books, research new techniques, and attend training sessions and seminars, which all contribute to the delivery of a professional and motivating coaching session.

It is the same with any passionate person, not just in a career sense but also in sports, hobbies and volunteering, if you're passionate you will live and breathe your passion and when people meet you, your passion will be conveyed as it rubs off on others and they to become quickly excited as they get caught up in the moment often through your tonality and expressions.

If you apply for a career that you are passionate about, a career you want to succeed in, you will automatically impress the interviewer as <u>your passion has to shine through.</u>

Customers will buy into almost any product that a sales assistant has to sell as long as it is sold with passion. Selling passionately works for all products from holidays to mobile phones, as long as the product's criterion closely or completely matches that of the customer's criteria. As the customer gets caught up in your passion, they will start to view you the product through excited eyes and when you feel excited about a product <u>you want it.</u>

One way to find your career passion is to match your personality to career ideas, you can <u>visit the Employment King website</u> for a free personality/career matching test <u>today,</u> or ask yourself what career would I do for free or what job would I pay to do?

As well as having passion you also need to be an expert in your career – this is such a powerful combination (passion and expertise) which will guarantee you more job offers, so here's how to become an industry expert....

Sales – The Dark Side of Psychology

1. Sell yourself throughout the interview
2. Understand the employer's criteria, highlight your benefits and reinforce your benefits through the use summary
3. Be aware that an employer will compare you to other candidates – ensure that you are not complacent and plan, prepare and deliver with passion – even if you think that the job is a done deal already.
4. Remember we all view the world differently; ensure the image you portray to the employer is positive
5. Highlight the value you will bring to the organisation
6. Only discuss your strengths throughout the interview
7. Be passionate about your career

The Expert Interview:

Influential Rules 9 to 14

Many people consider me to be an expert in passing job interviews due to my vast experience and training, but I have no training or experience in investment banking. The reason I mention this, is that I am looking for someone to transfer £10,000 in my bank so I can invest their money and hopefully earn you a good return, while I make a small profit. So – have I met a possible candidate in you, will you consider my offer?

I hope you won't and why would you as I have no experience, skills or knowledge in investment banking. But if you were looking to invest some money, who would you seek advice from? You would search for a financial expert as we all trust experts and professionals, we trust experts so much that we are willing to give them our life savings to invest with no guarantee of success or profit.

Remember you may attend a meeting with an "investment banker" but this title alone doesn't mean a thing, does it? How long has the person been an investment banker? A week, a month, twenty years? How successful is this person? What area of investment banking do they specialise in? We are all took in by titles and very rarely question what people tell us especially when we believe they are a professional or expert.

An experiment was carried out in a hospital, where a person posing as a doctor telephoned a ward nurse, stating that a certain patient urgently needed extra medication for their illness. In most cases the nurses willing complied and quickly headed in the direction of the medicine cabinet and the patient - the extra medication would have put the patient's lives in danger; the nurses were stopped by a second person who was part of the experiment. Nurses complied with authority, even when hospital procedures states that nurses cannot follow instructions given over the phone by doctors.

The same psychology works in a job interview, if you highlight your expertise and specialist knowledge, the interviewer will naturally trust you and with trust comes respect. Once the interviewer considers you an expert they will be willing to invest in you.

Rule No.9 MI5 Agent Technique

"We gain strength, and courage, and confidence by each experience in which we really stop to look fear in the face... we must do that which we think we cannot"
- Eleanor Roosevelt

To stand out in job interviews you need to be an expert in the industry of your choice, as employers respect expertise and know the profit making power of having an expert in their team.

As you already know, from an average of 300 people who originally applied for the job that only you and 5 other interviewees (on average) secured the opportunity to interview. This means that all 6 of you are strong candidates, so you need stand out from the crowd and possessing a talent or specific expertise will do this for you.

To win more job offers highlight the expertise you can bring to the company as this will give you a winning upper hand over other interviewees. Why? Who would you want to decorate your house, an expert or someone new to the field of painting or decorating? Who would you choose to operate on you; a doctor specialising in the field of your illness or a newly graduated doctor with only generalist knowledge?

The bottom line is <u>We Trust Experts</u>, we sometimes have to pay more for an expert and employers will offer higher wages when they require someone with a certain knowledge or skill – an expert.

A famous psychological experiment reinforces the potential power that an expert can exert over a non-expert. Milgram's experiment (1961) has been repeated several times with very similar results, it highlights how easily compliance and obedience can be achieved when individuals are assigned roles.

Two individuals (An actor and a genuine volunteer) were asked to participate in an experiment, believing that it was a study focused on memory. Which role the volunteer was assigned to was determined through drawing slips of paper, although this was rigged with the genuine volunteer always being assigned to the role of teacher rather than learner. The premise of the experiment is explained to the participants – that the teacher shall ask a series of questions relating to memory functions and if the learner answers incorrectly then they shall be punished through a shock administered by the teacher. It is explained that these shocks will be used to see how they impact on the answers given, i.e. If pain enhances memory function. It is also explained that the voltage for these shocks will increase in power as the experiment goes on.

During the experiment there is a scientist wearing a white science coat who is asking the volunteer to increase the voltage and administer the shocks, this scientist will reassure and encourage volunteers to administer increasing voltage levels, even as the volunteers can hear the experiment participant in the other room screaming in pain. Some volunteers continue to administer these volts even when the voltage they deliver states "Danger" and the actor volunteer has reached a point where they can no longer be heard screaming. The reassurance of the expert is so powerful and influential that the learner discounts their own view, placing trust in the expert knowledge of the man with a clipboard wearing a white coat. Just imagine the influence that you could wield with your expertise!

You won't always be applying for a job that you have an expert proficiency in, in some cases this may be an interview for the start of a new career. You can sell yourself and you can learn to sound like you know more then you know and I would add, by accessing the vast amount of information on the internet on your industry you can quickly speed up your learning.

To become NLP literate I didn't need to undertake the research project and modelling of experts that Grinder and Bandler - the founders of NLP completed. All I needed to do was locate, learn and put into practice the techniques and models that were the result of their many hours of research and study. Learning is best done when it is done quickly, when you read a book over a couple of days you quickly learn the message the author wanted you to grasp, but imagine reading this book one word a day , if you did this you wouldn't learn a single thing.

The more you read, research and talk about your industry and your career, the quicker you will become knowledgeable, leading to being an expert. Which is why it is so important for you to find a job your passionate about which matches your values, because this will allow you to enjoy reading and discussing your career.

You can become an expert by working in one industry for 10-20 years specialising in a certain niche or alternatively you can cheat and become or come across as "an expert" in just one week....

Rule No.10 Cheat the Interview

"You only live once, but if you do it right, once is enough."
— Mae West

You don't even have to be an expert to win job interviews you just need to come across as an expert – what is an expert anyway? It is just someone who can remember more about one subject or niche than others, so all you have to do is show you have this in-depth knowledge (don't worry you will learn how to remember vast amounts of information later using the Memory palace technique)

If you're passionate about the career and the industry you have chosen or you just want to pass your job interview, you need to become an **Industry Expert** and you can become an expert or sound like an expert in just one week.

An industry expert will have extensive knowledge about your career sector, the leading companies in this industry and the industry jargon employer's use.

7 Quick Steps to Cheat the Interview and become an Industry Expert in just One Week:

1. **Use A Search Engine:** Open a web search engine such as Google and in the search box write "Your industry name" and "Job profile" example "Web Designer Job Profile." Once you open a Job Profile, go down to the bottom of the page, as you will find links to industry websites such as the sector skills council websites. These websites are valuable and record a large amount of information and can be used to research the industry and future job trends.

2. **Match Your Skills to Your Career:** The job profile will also record the job duties, skills and qualities often required by employers. Highlight the skills and qualities you already possess and the duties you would enjoy undertaking if you were employed in this role. If you have highlighted at least 80% of these, you have found an industry that you should excel in, as the job duties already match the motivational part of your personality. While answering interview questions give examples of the skills you possess that are recorded on the job profile

3. **Set up Industry Alerts:** Set up Google alerts to receive relevant daily news feed, blog articles and website updates on the industry you are interested in applying for. You need to search for the following on Google Alerts then read and quote interesting and relevant aspects during your interview.

[Insert Job Title] **News**
E.g. Marketing Assistant/Accounts Manager/ Graduate Internship **News**

[Insert Job Industry] **Industry News**
E.g. Marketing /Accountancy/ Publishing/ Hospitality and Catering **Industry News**

[Insert Job Industry] **New Contracts and Funding**

E.g. Social care/Financial Services/ Beauty/ Public Services
New Contracts and Funding

4. **Twitter:** Follow "Industry" tweets to receive industry news feeds, industry job adverts and updates. Set up an "Industry" list. After a while Industry twitterers will search and add to you. Use twellow to search for twitters by industry. Don't be afraid to ask tweet questions to these people – even asking answers to potential interview questions, twitterers love to reply to tweets, they will feel flattered that you have picked them.

5. **Social Network Sites:** The social network sites for businesses is growing, join 3 of these such as LinkedIn and join industry forums, discussions and join in asking questions around the industry growth and decline and learn the meaning of industry jargon. Set up your own online industry profile-this needs to be a professional, polished page.

6. **Ask Facebook:** On Facebook search for "Friends" under "Co-workers", searching for them typing in their company name. You can befriend people working in your industry and then ask them questions or ask them to complete a questionnaire or poll - social networkers are normally keen to respond to this.

7. **Network:** Attend industry network events, always dress smart and be prepared to distribute your business card to other professionals. This is a great chance to update your industry information and meet industry leaders. Many job hunters establish productive links in this way and gain offers of employment or inside knowledge of when recruitment is upcoming.

With your research completed, and an increase in your industry knowledge and are now heading down the road to becoming an industry expert, to convince the interviewer of your new found expertise you need to communicate using the interviewers secret language...

Rule No.11 Learn the Secret Language of Interviews

"No one can make you feel inferior without your consent"
— Eleanor Roosevelt

Many people fail at interviews, due to the employer's repetitive use of industry jargon and the interviewee not understanding the meaning of these key abbreviations, acronyms and jargon. Unless you already know the industry you are applying for you first need to research industry terminology so you can use it during your job interview.

During the interview use the company specific acronyms and abbreviations used throughout your industry, your interviewer will automatically believe (through positive generalisation) that you are more experienced then perhaps you already are. **As only industry people understand industry the industry lingo** – as we covered earlier in the book we all generalise, delete and distort information.

When the interviewer mentions a piece of information that you have researched, agree and add to their sentence, as an example the interviewer might state that; **"There's been an increase in the use of X system."**

If you recently researched that company A has implemented X system, reply with **"Yes there has been an increase in companies using X system, I believe that company A recently spent £1 million implementing X system and in it's first year it has increased productivity by 5%, a great increase after an underachieving performance in the last financial year"**

By using snippets of information that you researched and by communicating using industry language, employers will quickly filter this information making a snap decision that you are at the minimum knowledgeable in the sector or at best, an expert in the industry.

The key to becoming an industry expert is research, but understanding what to detect will save you hours of wasted time, while keeping you focused on the key points the employer is interested in....

Rule No.12 Secret Detective

"Insanity is doing the same thing, over and over again, but expecting different results" — Albert Einstein

In the age of the internet, we have the luxury of being able to research companies with ease. If you really wanted to you could complete this on your way to the interview using your smart phone. At this point we don't recommend this – that is until you master The Memory Palace exercise that you will learn in an additional chapter, but what is the key to research?

The internet is a great resource due to the large amount of information we can access at the touch of a button, don't you agree? This great amount of information is also the downside to research as you can quickly get bogged down with the amount of information websites and blogs offer.

The key to effectual research, as a detective knows is what to research - this way you can target your search terms to gather only relevant information.

Research the company- before any interview, research the company as you will often be asked the question **"What do you know about our company?"** Be sure to include the company history in your research, this can often be found on the company's website.

Local Market Information- LMI; Is your industry on the increase or decline in terms of progression? If the industry is on the decline you might need to rethink your career ideas or to move to an area where the industry is on the rise. What government policies affect your industry? What is the predicted growth for your sector? What countries and UK locations recruit for your industry or buy your industry's product?

The changing future - Industries are changing at a fast pace, due to the improvements in technology, it is always positive to show the employer you know how the industry has changed from its original origins and how the industry is going to develop in the future. What direction is your industry heading in as new technologies and world competition change the way each industry works?

Discussing the changing future for the industry not only backs up your industry knowledge and expertise but highlights your passion for this career – and <u>passionate people make the best workers.</u>

Through your research (especially through the information that you will gather through signing up to Google feeds) you will collect a large amount of industry information in just a couple of days. It is unlikely that you will be able to read all of this information so you must skim through and record key reoccurring points, taking note of the origin and source to ensure credibility. Credibility and accuracy are important if you plan to use specific figures in your interview, you don't want to quote wrong information as this will quickly break the image of you being an industry expert.

To back up your expertise you need show you posses the required skills for the position, direct experience is the best way to do this. Rule 13 will teach you how to highlight your transferrable skills, even when you have required them from a different job sector...

Rule No.13 Undersell Yourself at Your Peril

"Twenty years from now you will be more disappointed by the things that you didn't do than by the ones you did do"
— Mark Twain

When recruiting, employers will have a list of essential criteria required for each position; if you meet these criteria during the job interview you will be offered the position.

Through your industry research you have started to discover what skills and qualities the employer requires for your job position, the next step is to ensure you can relate a real life or work experience to each required skill or quality as this is the basis of your interview answers.

First read the job specification or job profile and write down all the required skills and qualities both essential and desirable.

We never truly know which questions we are going to be asked; the job specification tells us the type of person the employer is looking for, from this we can confidently presume that the questions will be based on the essential criteria recorded on the job specification.

Job Specification

Telesales Executive, Responsible to the Sales manager

Essential Criteria:

Previous experience of meeting targets
Example Interview question: *"Have you ever worked in a role where you have had set targets to meet?"*

Excellent communication skills
Example Interview question: *"Give an example of when you have used communication skills to calm down an irate or difficult customer"*

Take your Job Specification and under each Essential Criteria, write a potential question that may be used by interviewers in order to test each of these competencies.

Tips for preparing what interview questions you may be asked:

- If you know someone who works for the company you are applying to work for, ask them what questions they were asked; first check if their job role is different to the one you are applying for, as the interviewer will use a different set of questions for the various positions.

- Join a social networking site, search for members working in your industry and ask them for example interview questions and answers, you will find that many social network site users are happy to share their knowledge and advice.

- Think back to questions that you are have been asked in previous job interviews. Interviewers often use generic questions in order to obtain as much information as possible about the kind of worker you are.

Pre interview preparation is essential – before the interview, you need to be fully aware of <u>your own key skills and strengths</u>, once identified you will need to be able to sell these skills and strengths in order to secure you your new job, using the **3 Steps to Selling Anything** you learnt earlier on.

To start your preparation look at the list of Skills, Qualities, Strengths and Career Successes you recorded earlier. Compare your list of skills, against the essential criteria skills from the job specification and highlight all the skills you possess from your list that match those on the job specification.

Now, look at the essential criteria skills that you have <u>not highlighted</u>. The fact that you haven't listed these competencies doesn't necessarily mean that they are not within your capabilities; it may be that these are simply not in the forefront of your mind. However it is essential that you prepare answers and examples to fulfil these parts of the specification.

You need to ensure that you believe you have the skills you have not circled, as you will be asked about these skills during the job interview and coming across confidently is one of the key aspects to winning job offers. Write down each skill and break down the skill into smaller *chunks*. Ask yourself **"What is this skill? How can it be broken down into different tasks, attributes, responsibilities?"**

As an example: Communication Skills – *liaising with colleagues, welcoming clients, constructing letters, corresponding with professionals over email*

Let your imagination go with this - the more possibilities you produce, the better.

From these you can then pinpoint those which you think would be most relevant. If you are struggling to find many examples, a simple but often overlooked technique can be used to help you clear your mind and ease the flow of ideas.

1. **Close your eyes and think of a white screen, imagining it to be large, about the size of a cinema screen**

2. **Take 3 three deep inhalations and 2 long exhalations.**

3. **Then repeat your question out loud 'How do I (time manage)? The answers will appear on the white screen in front of you now.**

Re-read the job specification, write down, on a separate piece of paper all the <u>essential skills</u> needed for the position you are applying for:

- **Teamwork**
- **Communication Skills**
- **Problem Solving**
- **Supervisory Skills**

Next to each skill make a note of how a previous experience of yours has used this skill or quality, this example will highlight a transferrable skill from a hobby.

Example:

Teamwork – "I play for a football team with my friends"

Re-write your answers two more times, adding additional information to turn your experience into a small paragraph, edit your answers until they are perfect. You now have the basis of your interview questions and answers.

Teamwork – "I am an excellent team player; each week I play 5-aside football and I understand how as a team you can achieve more."

Teamwork – "My experience of playing 5-aside football has taught me the value of what teamwork can achieve. As a team member you have the opportunity to share everyone's ideas and experiences, which is a great resource. If a team member is feeling down the rest of team will motivate the individual ensuring everyone performs at their best."

With a list of skills (the questions asked during the interview will relate to the essential criteria and skills needed for the position) you now have a better awareness of the interview questions you will be asked, by completing the above exercises, you now have your answers prepared. Some additional pointers to help you during the question and answer session are:

- **Use stories to sell yourself and to highlight your transferable skills**

- **Never give just a "Yes" or "No" answer – expand and voluntarily offer demonstrable evidence without being prompted – make it easy for the interviewer and take control as the expert.**

- **When possible quote quantifiable figures and percentages – these may be from your industry research or it may be figures specific to your performance.**

- **Quote past positive comments by others – these may be from your line management, clients, customers, inspectors, auditors etc.**

Finally, to ensure you present yourself well and come across confidently take the opportunity to practice on a friend or ideally a professional Careers Advisor who can carry out a mock interview with you using the questions you have prepared. This will help you with the timing of your answers, re-writing answers that don't sell you and overcoming nerves - as they say *practice makes perfect.*

As you are becoming better informed about your industry, you are also becoming more aware of your skills and strengths. Your research has taught you the industry routes and the predicted future of your sector but sometimes you still need to play it safe, you need to word answers in interviews with an element of ambiguity, until you can work out what type of employer is interviewing you....

Rule No.14 Wear a Condom

"Live as if you were to die tomorrow. Learn as if you were to live forever." — Mahatma Gandhi

Governments continue to highlight the importance of wearing a condom, especially when making love to a stranger - they want you play it safe, not to take unnecessary risks. This awareness should be considered in the job interview, why take a risk when you can play it safe?

The more you read through this book the more you will learn about reading people, soon you will able to quickly workout a person's personality and motivational traits within a couple of minutes of meeting them, which means you can alter your language to influence them. But when you first meet an interviewer, you may want to play the safe ground and remain neutral until you know what to say to persuade them to recruit you.

Some high level managers are set in their ways and enjoy using techniques and tactics that that are tried and tested, while other managers pride themselves on their dynamism and are always on the lookout for new ways of working, embracing new technologies, systems and processes.

Hopefully if you have your own preference, you will have applied for a company with your same values. If you're the type of person who will fit in with any company and YOU just want a job, play the middle and safe ground.

Play it safe - when asked an options question **"What do you think about using X technology (new) compared to using x (old) system?"** To answer safely give positive and negative examples for both ways of thinking **"Well, the new technology will A, B and C (positive) but may XXX (negative) while the old system does A, B and C (positive) but has proven to XXX (negative).**

This first highlights your industry knowledge and illustrates your ability to look at the *bigger picture* and more importantly you maintain rapport with the interviewer by matching their values and employers will often give away what they value during the interview. I would add that if you match the employer's values you will have instant rapport and instant rapport is equal to a successful interview.

I agree to be successful in job interviews you have be an expert in the job, career or the sector you are working in and you have to understand sales techniques to ensure the employer is focused on your positive selling points not your negatives, but to really achieve a successful interview you need to overcome interview anxiety and be confident...

The Expert Interview

1. People trust experts
2. Use social media to improve your industry knowledge
3. Research if necessary and understand industry jargon and terminology
4. Highlight your knowledge of industry growth
5. Beware of the skills you require which are needed in the position you are applying for
6. Give safe answer to ambiguous questions until you understand the employer's values

Commanding Confidence:

Influential Rules 15 to 23

As a coach I have worked with a variety of people from all backgrounds from CEOs to teenagers, enabling a boost in their confidence. All my clients start by telling me that they have no confidence (and they are normally confident about that fact) and that they have never been a confident person. As I explore with them their lives, interest and careers I often find that clients are confident in certain aspects of their lives but are lacking in others. Remember we all generalise, if you feel you're not a confident person you need to be specific – what are you not a confident person at? And more important in what situations are you confident?

To pass any interview you need to be confident, even as you learn influential language patterns and how to become an industry expert, none of these techniques will work unless you feel confident and I would add the more you learn these influencing techniques the more confident you will become at using them in job interviews and in everyday life.

What is confidence? Confidence is **"Believing In Yourself"** It's a state just like happiness, stress, joy, anger or love. As with all states we can control your confidence levels and with a little training you can access a Confident State whenever we need to.

I tell my clients, when you feel confident you walk, stand, talk (including self-talk) and act differently. By knowing the difference between how you act as a confident and nervous you, in terms of your posture, body language, belief system and language pattern you can train your brain to feel confident whenever you please.

Imagine you were a confident interviewee, how would this change the way you presented yourself? You are probably already thinking of the thousands of ways you can use your confident state in all the areas of your life, but how long does it take to become a confident person? 10 years, 5 year, 1 year, a month, a week? No just 5 minutes!

Rule No.15 Not Cocky But Confident

"To be yourself in a world that is constantly trying to make you something else is the greatest accomplishment."
— Ralph Waldo Emerson

Our mind works best when it learns quickly; we don't need to spend years in the office of a psychiatrist, lying on a couch talking about what made you nervous to help you overcome your fears of interviews, public speaking, spiders or heights. You can learn to be confident really quickly by focusing on you as a confident person and the outcome you will achieve when you <u>feel confident</u>.

Clear your mind and imagine you were a really confident person, if you could see yourself as a confident person how would the confident you be standing? View this confident person as if you were in the room watching a confident version of yourself. What would the posture of the confident you look like, how would you hold yourself, how would you tilt your head? Now, your turn - stand in this confident way, take on the posture of this confident you. Do this now.

Become aware of everything a confident you would do, notice how you breath when you feel confident, how do you walk and stand, what do you say to yourself? How do you feel? Where does the confident feeling come from inside you? What direction does confidence feeling flow through your body? If you could give it a colour and temperature, what would it be?

As you become aware of all the elements that make you feel confident, as you see, feel and hear yourself as a confident person you will <u>start to feel confident</u> right now.

In your mind's eye, see this confident version of you, <u>watch you being confident, now</u> stand up and walk around this confident you, so you unconsciously become aware of everything that makes you feel confident. Walk behind this confident you and step into your confident body, see the world through the eyes of you feeling confident; see what you can see, hear what you can hear - <u>now you feel confident</u> and imagine how that confident emotion feels, running through your body.

Take a deep breath in and REPEAT this process.

Remember this new learning and experience, which you will use to <u>feel confident during your next job interview</u>. Just by imagining that you are confident, can help you feel confident and after a bit of repetition this confident feeling will be instilled into your unconsciousness. Practice this exercise everyday for 5-10 days and you will start to feel more and more confident each and every day in preparation for your job interview.

You feel more confident already which means you have taught your brain to change quickly and a quick change means you can learn more quickly. You will also learn why some people look forward to the pleasure of a job interview while other candidates hate the thought of the pain of a job interview, but this just depends on how you can control your perspective......

Rule No.16 Pain and Pleasure

"Life is what happens to you while you're busy making other plans." — John Lennon

Why do some people look forward to job interviews (that's right some people actually love job interviews!) while other people panic at the mere thought? For some, the feeling of pain is so intense that they actually flee rather than facing up to the process.

To pass any job interview you have to <u>feel confident</u>, the reason some people succumb to those dreaded interview nerves is due to how they imagine the interview in their mind, you will associate either Pain or Pleasure to the thought of the job interview!

Close your eyes and think about an upcoming job interview – what is happening in the video playing in your mind? Do you see a negative version or a positive version of the interview? I anticipate that you are playing a negative version in your mind.

I would also guess that when you thought about this negative film in your mind's eye, the image was a large coloured film and when you feel at your most nervous, you are probably seeing the film from the eyes of the you in the film, creating a deep association that makes you feel nervous and scared?

I know this because this type of negative image is a common one that stops thousands of people passing job interviews and here is how to break that pattern:

1. **First if the image is a film – Pause the film.**

2. **Place a large frame around the picture, an old thick frame like you might find in an old style art gallery**

3. **Change the colour picture to black and white - how do you feel now? Less nervous?**

4. **Be aware of where your image is in your mind's eye and slowly move that image further and further away from your mind, further and further away, making the image smaller and smaller, notice as the image decreases in size, the negative emotions decrease in power**

5. **Push the image towards the horizon and as the image moves away from you the picture is distorted and hard to see. Keep this image heading away from you until it's a dot and until the dot vanishes. Have all your negative feeling disappeared?**

6.   **Repeat this exercise 5 more times and notice how each time you complete this exercise the image of the job interview is less powerful**

Next I want you to imagine in your mind's eye that you are attending a job interview that is going really well, a job interview that for whatever reason no matter what you say or do the interviewer is really impressed.

Search for that image in your mind's eye, for some it will be hard to find which means you need to close your eyes and let the image come to you, now. For many people this positive interview image may look like it is far away in the distance of the quality of this image may be poor, the picture may be blurred, but all I want you to do is locate the image no matter where it is in your mind's eye and I know you can find it now.

You will now learn what confident interviewees see in their minds eye:

1.   **Once you have located your image in your mind's eye, bring that image closer and closer – all the way until the image is so large that it is all you can see in your mind's eye. Do this slowly at first and notice the closer you bring your image the clearer the image becomes, until you appreciate all of the detail of that picture**

2.   **Turn this picture into a coloured image**

3.   **Imagine you had a magic remote control, that can turn pictures into movies – press play and turn your interview picture into a movie; and this movie shows you at your very best, impressing the interviewer. Watch this movie from the beginning to the end.**

4.   **Re-watch this movie a second time and this time use your remote control to turn up the volume so that you can hear**

every detail of what is being said. Hear the tone of your voice, the positive self talk and the laughter from the bond you and the interviewer have created.

5. Re-watch the movie for a third time, but this time I want you to step into the movie so you can play the movie from the point of view of the you in the movie. This way you can see what you can see as <u>you are there in the interview room, now,</u> you can hear what you can hear and you can feel all those positive emotions you have from being in a confident and successful interview

6. Complete this exercise 3-4 times

We attach emotions to the images we create in our mind and it is obvious that if you make a negative image you will feel negative emotions but when you create big positive pictures you feel positive emotions. By changing the submodalities (the size of the image, the colour, the sound, the distance the picture is in your mind), and how you view this image (from an observer or the eyes of the you in the image) alters how you feel about the image you first created.

Creating positive interview pictures in your mind will let you feel motivated, the Online Coaching Course by Employment King uses a variety of similar techniques to help you delete fears and increase confidence and they all come down to changing how you perceive the situation, but to make real long-lasting changes you need to change your personal limiting beliefs.....

Rule No.17 Limit the Limiting Beliefs

"There are only two ways to live your life. One is as though nothing is a miracle. The other is as though everything is a miracle."
— Albert Einstein

In order to move forward you need to understand your own beliefs and which beliefs are limiting and which beliefs are empowering.

Fill in the blanks:

- I am _____ at job interviews

- I am _____ when talking about my strengths

- **During job interviews I will often feel _____**

What do you believe about your interview skills? Do you believe you are confident or nervous? Do you believe that you deserve a job offer or do you believe that someone better will be offered the job?

Limiting beliefs are powerful as your mind will focus on your internal conversations, which leads to limiting beliefs becoming self fulfilling prophecies. If you truly believe you are shy and under confident in job interviews, your subconscious will concentrate on this belief making you act shy and under confident.

Pick one of your limiting beliefs – why do you believe this statement? Because in your mind you have backed this belief up with evidence, haven't you? If you challenge the evidence <u>you will break your belief</u>.

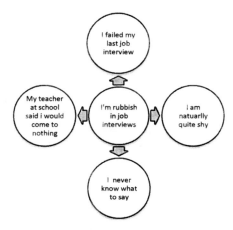

To change your beliefs, question and challenge the evidence that backs up your limiting belief, look for the generalisations, check to see what is missing – essentially create doubt in your belief.

My Teacher at School said I would come to nothing –
- What else did your teacher say that didn't come true
- Can your teacher predict everyone's future accurately?
- Are you a different person from the child your School Teacher knew?

I never know what to say –
- When where you last asked a question that you quickly responded well to?
- Which interview questions do you answer well?
- What do you enjoy talking about?

As you can see, once you start questioning your limiting beliefs you will start to create doubt which will lead to you changing your beliefs.

Write down each of your limiting beliefs one by one and the evidence you use to back up this belief:

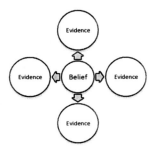

Evidence 1:
Record 3 questions that you can ask yourself to challenge this belief

1. _____
   _____
   _____

2. _____
   _____
3. _____
   _____
   _____

Evidence 2:
Record 3 questions that you can ask yourself to challenge this belief

1. _____
   _____
2. _____
   _____
3. _____
   _____
   _____

Evidence 3:
Record 3 questions that you can ask yourself to challenge this belief

1. _____
   _____
2. _____
   _____
3. _____
   _____
   _____

Evidence 4:
Record 3 questions that you can ask yourself to challenge this belief

1. _____
   _____
2. _____
   _____
3. _____
   _____
   _____

Take your limiting beliefs and update them, giving yourself a new opportunity.

Limiting Belief	Updated Belief
Example:	
I always make mistakes	I always learn from anything that does not go to plan
Interviews are hard	Interviews get easier the more I practice them
I'm rubbish at job interviews	I'm confident in job interviews when I have prepared for them

Add your limiting and updated beliefs below: How you would like to be!

Limiting Belief	Updated Belief

Now you have a list of new beliefs, but beliefs only work when we truly believe them, as an example before 1945 people believed that **you could not run a mile in under 4 minutes,** this was a belief that everyone shared which meant it was an easy belief to back up with evidence (other people and athletes telling you – your evidence does not need to be true for you to use it to back up your belief) athletes attempted to run a mile in under 4 minutes and failed.

In 1945 Roger Banister ran a mile in under 4 minutes instantly breaking that belief, the following year 37 other runners ran a mile in under 4 minutes – that's the power of beliefs.

Record your new positive belief and look for evidence to back up your belief and I would add, once you find evidence to back up your new belief you will truly believe, which will result in the belief becoming a reality.

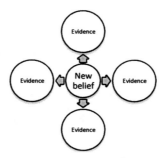

Your beliefs are powerful, as you already know you will search for evidence to back up your beliefs; be certain that your new beliefs have a positive purpose, re-read your new beliefs and say them out loud. Imagine yourself living your new beliefs feeling more positive about moving forward.

As you are learning about gaining new confidence and breaking limiting beliefs you will start to feel like a new positive you. You will also learn that our mind adapts and picks things up quickly and that you can take something that someone else has learnt over a vast period and acquire it yourself quickly – we call this modelling and you can learn to model confident people....

Rule No.18 Steal Confidence From Others

"To live is the rarest thing in the world. Most people exist, that is all." — Oscar Wilde

To accelerate your confidence and improve your resources, you can easily learn from others, taking the confidence they have learnt over a vast period of time and mastering it yourself in minutes. In the **online coaching course** we show you several modelling techniques; the one you will learn today is one of my personal favourite exercises that I constantly use in pursuit of my own personal and professional self development. Modelling is a process in which we adopt certain behaviours and skills, understanding the thought processes behind them and using these to our advantage in any aspect we need to within our lives.

First pick someone you know who is really confident, ideally when they are faced with an interview situation. When modelling confidence you don't need to discuss the interview question answers your model uses, it's more important to understand what is going on internally which means by understanding how your model sees the world, you can access their model for confidence.

Questions	Models Answers
Environment Where and when do you feel confident?	
Behaviours What specifically do you do to feel confident? If you were going to teach me to be confident in job interviews, what would you ask me to do?	
Capabilities What skills do you have that enable you to feel confident? How did you learn how to do this?	

Beliefs	
What do you believe about yourself when you're feeling confident? What do you believe about the person/environment you're doing this to/in?	
Identity	
What is your personal mission or vision when you're a confident interviewee?	
More Questions	
How do you know that you're good at interviews? What emotional and physical state are you in when you do this? What happened for you to be good at this? What are you trying to achieve when you do this? Who else do you recommend I talk to about this?	

Experience has a structure, by asking your model the logical questions you will gain a real insight into your models map of their world – in most cases your model won't even be aware of the structure of their skill, as they carry out this skill unconsciously.

Example modelling question and answer:

Logical Level Questions	Models Answers
Environment	I start to feel confident as soon as I see the interviewer, before this I still feel a slight nervousness.
Where and when do you feel	

confident?	The confident feeling starts in my stomach and feels warm, this quickly spreads out around my body
Behaviours What specifically do you do to feel confident? If you were going to teach me to be confident in job interviews, what would you ask me to do?	I first smile and introduce myself by checking the employers first reactions of me (which are positive as I look the part and gave a professional introduction) my confidence grows. In my head I visualise what I am going to say, how I will act and how the employer will react to me and as this happens in real life it builds on my confidence
Capabilities What skills do you have that enable you to feel confident? How did you learn how to do this?	I have passed interviews before and I know I am good at my job, I use this knowledge to give myself positive self talk I learnt to be confident in interviews because I enjoy talking to people
Beliefs What do you believe about yourself when you're feeling confident? What do you believe about the person/environment you're doing this to/in?	I 100% believe I will be offered a job, this is not to be big-headed but this belief ensures that I am able to focus, I listen to the questions and offer considered answers I also believe the interviewer will like me as I am good at building rapport
Identity	I would say my mission is to be

What is your personal mission or vision when you're a confident interviewee?	offered the job but more likely my mission is to get the interviewer to be so impressed they never have a doubt in their mind that I am the person they are looking for
More Questions How do you know that you're good at interviews? What emotional and physical state are you in when you do this? What happened for you to be good at this? What are you trying to achieve when you do this? Who else do you recommend I talk to about this?	As I believe I am a good worker this automatically gives me confidence – I can actually feel that confident feeling in my body throughout the interview and I keep visualising positive outcomes to my questions and answers I would recommend visualising your positive job interview before the actual interview

The logical levels questions are a guide, it's not about which questions you use, the aim is to elicit the details of your role models strategy which means you need to ask questions to gain the details - **it's all in the details!!!**

Let's re-look at one of the answers, what other questions could you ask to really understand your models map of their world?

Behaviours What specifically do you do?	**I first smile and introduce myself by checking the employers first reactions of me**

	(which are positive as I look the part and gave a professional introduction) my confidence grows. In my head I visualise what I am going to say, how I will act and how the employer will react to me and as this happens in real life it builds on my confidence
Additional Questions to elicit Detail • Do you smile or visualise first? • Is your visualisation a picture or a film? • Is it colour or black and white • From what point of view do you see the film from • How important is this visualising?	I use the visualisations before the interview and during it. Before meeting the employer I create a big colourful film that I can see from the point of view of the me in the film (it actually feels like I am there) it is a really positive image with the interview going well, there is always lots of chatting and laughing and the image makes me feel confident instantly

Modelling is a very successful way of quickly gaining or learning a new skill, use each logical level as a guide to ask detailed questions about your role model and their strategy, once you have learnt the breakdown of their skill all you need to do is follow their strategy and you will have the same result – try it, this technique is very effective

- **The questions on beliefs and values are highly important, as an example, when someone believes that they have to win no matter what. This belief will drive them forward, not allowing mistakes to get them down**

- Ask your model, "What are you saying to yourself when you do X?" this type of question can undercover a person's beliefs, values and their identity

- By modelling someone's beliefs and values when they complete a task, you will change the way you act/perform which will have a subsequently impact on the outcome

With this new learnt confidence you are feeling more prepared for your next job interview; confidence is seen through a person's body language, gestures and language, and often a confident person will have a flow to their voice...

Rule No.19 Give Your Voice a Boost

"That which does not kill us makes us stronger."
— Friedrich Nietzsche

Interviewers will listen consciously to your words and the interview answers to consciously decide if you're the right person for this particular position, but more importantly the interviewer will often have a gut feeling if you're the right person for this job - **unconsciously.**

You use your voice to create sounds and your listener will use your voice to decide what type of person you are, this can often be wrong as we make snap judgements, but I would add once a person has made up their mind about you even when they have the wrong opinion it is hard to change it as people are influenced by their own commitment that they have made.

In an interview you can use your voice to portray your character, to attach different emotions to your words or to encourage the listener to listen more intently. With your voice you can mutter, whisper, or shout. You can roar, suggest or demand. You can state, announce, assert, declare, affirm – your voice can command the interviewer and is the key to how your words are filtered by the employer.

Picture yourself at country fair and on the cake stall you spot two large cakes, the two ladies manning the stalls are selling slices at an equal price for charitable organisations. In the spirit of charity or perhaps to increase sales they were giving away free samples. After tasting each sample you decide that both cakes had been made to equal levels of taste. But you notice that one cake is selling much quicker than the other, in fact it appears to be selling three times faster than the other. You are confused, you step in for a closer look and notice that one cake is packaged in a bespoke patterned box, the other is packaged in a plain cardboard box. You realise that it was this, the presentation, the first impression that made the difference. You now have to make the choice, which will you pick, a cake packaged in a beautiful box or a second cake equally as tasty boxed in a plain white box?

We would all buy the beautifully packaged boxed, as the box represents the worth of the cake. Your voice is the package for your words, two people can use the same selling line or answer but the tone you say those words in can alter how the interviewer interprets them.

5 Interview Voice Tips

1. Vary the elements of your voice, allow your voice to rise and fall throughout the interview using your voice to portray emotions such as excitement and enthusiasm – remember that a monotone voice suggest to the interviewer that you have little interest in them, the job and the interview

2. Change the pace of your voice talking faster when discussing successes and slower when communicating key pieces of information such as how you will achieve targets and objectives

3. Add expressions while communicating as this will carry in your voice. One single sentence can have many meanings

depending on your expression and voice tone. Take this example:

"My last manager said I was a good worker"

The meaning of this sentence will be interpreted by the employer differently depending **on your voice tone/expression**

Read the same sentence and raise your voice on the bolder text

"My last manager said **I was a good worker**"
"**My last manager said** I was a good worker"

The first sentence sounds as if you are joking, my manger thought I was a good worker but I'm not. While the second sentence sounds as if you're trying to prove a point, I am a good worker because my manger said so. How you control your voice impacts on the meaning you portray.

4. Raise the volume gradually as you build towards a point and lower your voice when you are confident that you have achieved rapport to motivate the interviewer to listen more intently to you.

5. Use a rhythm when communicating a large amount of information, as singers do in songs, this allows the interviewer to stay in your flow and then pause to allow the interviewer to absorb the information or just before you move on to a second point

All the techniques we have used so far are designed to help increase your self-belief and confidence, but I would also like to add that too much confidence can be a disadvantage as you also need to feel some nervous to get into "The Zone"....

Rule No.20 Show Your Nerves, Confidently

"You've gotta dance like there's nobody watching, Love like you'll never be hurt, Sing like there's nobody listening, and live like it's heaven on earth." — William W. Purkey

As discussed in an earlier chapter when we meet someone we quickly put the person into a group by unconsciously assessing them, on the basic level we want to know if this new person is to be feared (a danger) or liked (a potential mate). When under attack (the person is a danger or threat) we have an automatic response to **flight or fight**, this is a survival tactic.

Flight — we all get that urge when confronted with a potentially embarrassing or difficult situation to run away from it, this happens in all areas of our lives from not attending a job interview because you don't want others to perceive you as a failure if you fail to secure the position, to delivering large presentations. I have encountered people who have turned on their heel and literally ran away from these pressured and threatening situations. Our ancestors would use **flight** when confronted by large predators, so does this mean the fastest runners survive the longest?

Fight — you go for it, many will visualise themselves doing well at the task or activity, or even when they feel they may fail they say to themselves **"go for it"** and jump in feet first which can often end with a positive result. Our ancestors would use the fight response to fight off neighbouring tribes who wanted to loot their village.

When confronted with a potential fight or flight situation our body produces a large amount of adrenalin to supply us with a burst of energy to engage in either fight or flight. Some of us fight as we have made a commitment and don't want to let others down; some will fight because they can't see a way out (to flight).

We will all come across challenging events, which means you can learn how to cope with them. Once you know how cope with challenging events, you will have the power to move forward with your life, helping you overcome any new challenge using all your emotions; confidence and nervousness – as you need both of these to be successful.

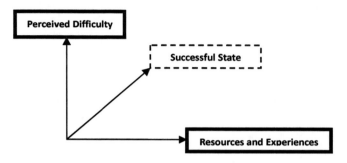

Perceived Difficulty; when thinking about your future interview, if you perceive the interview to be too difficult and you imagine yourself failing and due the perceived difficulty you will quickly become stressed and anxious. In this state you are probably already packing your bags getting ready for **"flight."** It is important not to go to the other extreme, if you believe that an interview will be a breeze or too easy, then the apathy will be communicated to the interviewers, doing you no favours. When interviews or job roles are too easy you will quickly become bored and boredom in a job/interview leads to one thing – no effort or enthusiasm.

Resources and Experiences; on the opposite axis; you may have completed so many job application forms and attended many job interviews that you have all the resources you need, this can lead to you becoming stale, bored and careless, this state can lead long-term to depression (more so in life and career situations then in job interviews as they are few and generally spaced out in time). Having no resources (which can include experiences, books, list of interview questions) to rely on can lead to panic.

Successful State; we all need a mix of perceived difficulty to keep you on your toes and resources/experiences, to back us up. When I deliver group sessions I feel nervous before stepping out in front of a big audience, this helps me to stay motivated, if I delivered sessions without these nerves I would become quickly bored. If the nervousness rises to outside of my comfort zone and I feel that it is having a counterproductive effect then I can use my previous experiences to remind me that I get great feedback from my course delegates and use exercises that have worked to get my point across. I also know I have resources prepared that I can use when needed. Both being nervous and prepared helps me **stay in the Successful State.**

To succeed in job interviews you need to access your successful state, you need to feel positive and confident as well as feeling a little apprehension. You can use the techniques in this book, your past interview experiences and the practice of your interview questions to build up your resources as well as feeling a little nervous (but mainly confidence) to **access your success state**, giving you a winning formula.

Those who struggle with interviews often talk to themselves negatively, hearing a voice in their head saying **"You can't do it"**, but if you suffer from a little gremlin in your head putting you down, it is time to kick him out, so flick over the page and I will I teach you how to get rid of your negative self talk.....

Rule No.21 Playing With the Devil

"Be yourself; everyone else is already taken."
— Oscar Wilde

Many people are let down by their own self talk – the devil in their head, it's bad enough when other people limit our beliefs by telling us we can't do this or we will fail at that, but to let our own self talk put you down is criminal.

Saying that though, we all have and use our negative self talk and negative self talk can really paralyse a person's self-confidence, creating the negative interview image we discussed before. The trick is to be aware of when this negative self-talk starts and then just turn the volume down as you will agree a loud voice saying **"You can't do it"** is more likely to convince you then a quiet voice you can hardly hear.

This technique takes 4-5 minutes and once practised can easily de-power the powerful negative self talk voice

- **Think back to a time when you crippled yourself with some negative self talk. Notice, where this voice is? Is it on the left or the right hand side of your head? In the front or the back of your mind?**
- **How loud is the voice? Normal, softer or louder – become aware of what make this voice negative?**
- **If you could turn this voice into a shape, what shape would it be? A square, Triangle, Circle or any other shape? What shape is your voice? If you can't turn the voice into a shape, imagine you were someone who could turn the voice into a shape – what shape is your voice?**
- **What colour is your shape? Is the shape in the same place the voice was?**
- **Slowly move the shape away from your head, down towards your shoulder, how does it feel now – most say it feels less powerful, amazing, hey?**
- **Allow the shape to move from your shoulder down your arm towards your elbow, how does it feel now, is the negative emotion vanishing? Yes?**
- **Let the shape continue further down from your elbow to your hand, notice how your negative emotions losses strength the further down the shape goes, move the shape to your leg, at its own speed allow the shape to drop down from your leg to your knee – how does it feel now? Less powerful?**
- **Move it from your knee to your foot, is the negative feeling vanishing? With the shape on your foot, how do you feel, more positive?**

- Finally allow the shape to fall onto the floor – what do you want to do to the shape? Kick it away? Stamp on it? Put it under your chair?
- Move the shape so you can't see it, now how do you feel, have all the negative emotions vanished? Most said they vanished a long time ago. How easy and amazing is this exercise?
- Try this exercise 3 times and notice how it gets easier and quicker to remove the negative voice each time you try it.

How great was that technique? For some they don't only hear negative voices but they have memories from past failed interviews that keep re-appearing like a video replaying over and over again, but like with negative voices your mind can evolve by destroying these painful interview memories...

Rule No.22 Destroy Painful Interview Memories

"If your ship doesn't come in, swim out to meet it"
— Jonathan Winters

You may or may not have a phobia of interviews but when you think back to negative interview memories you may feel a bit of discomfort, scared, nervous or have butterflies. To perform at your optimum during job interviews you need to delete these negative emotions forever.

This technique can be used alone or if you have a phobia you can add part 2 and 3 to part 7 of the phobia removal exercise that you will learn next

1. Think of job interviews and become aware of what image and film comes to your mind, notice the images and sounds that come to mind as the movie plays out in your mind's eye
2. Pause this image and put to one side, next select a theme tune that mismatches the negative interview film, I use the

Benny hill theme tune, as upbeat music works well with this exercise

3. Change the interviewer into a cartoon character and like all cartoon characters exaggerate the interviewers funny features; if the interviewer had a big nose then scale up the cartoon nose, so it look's massive

4. Rewind the interview film to the beginning and play the movie again, with the fun music playing nice and loud and with the interviewer as a cartoon character throughout the whole film

5. Again rewind the interview film and replay the movie but this time without the music or cartoon and notice how different you feel. Have your unpleasant feelings gone? If not repeat this exercise 3-4 times

Most people before an interview, who haven't used and practiced the techniques above, will feel nervous or anxious but some people will go one step further and have an actual phobia of interviews. I know to those of us who don't have an interview phobia a phobia can seem silly, so silly that you can laugh at your phobia.

I've met people with a phobia of all sorts of things I once knew a person with a phobia of pencils, imagine that - you can't pick up a pencil, you can't even look at a pencil. Phobias are in the mind of the beholder and can be laughed at, you can feel the urge to laugh at your phobia now by changing the submodalities of the phobic image as we did with the confidence image at an earlier sessions...

Rule No.23 Fast Interview Phobia Removal Technique

"Fairy tales are more than true; not because they tell us that dragons exist, but because they tell us that dragons can be beaten."
— G.K. Chesterton

If you have a real fear of interviews, not just a feeling of anxiousness but I mean a real phobia, then none of the language and influencing techniques you will shortly learn in this book will help, until you **remove your phobia**. This next technique will help you eliminate your phobia in a matter of minutes for ever. Read through the exercise first and repeat it three or four times embedding it into your unconsciousness.

1. In your mind's eye, imagine walking into a cinema and see everything you can see from the eyes of the you in the cinema, imagine you are there now, what can you smell, what can you hear and what can you see?

2. Walk into the cinema seating area and choose a seat in the front row of the cinema, as you walk in you notice you are alone. The film you are going to watch is a film of you in a job interview, as you look up at the screen you can see a still image of yourself in black and white, before your interview phobia incident took place – this <u>is a safe place</u> before you become phobic

3. Next, imagine floating up and out of your body, as you float up, head towards the projection room at the back of the cinema, once there you can view yourself in the cinema waiting to watch the you on the screen

4. Remaining in the projection room watch yourself watching the you in the interview - press the play button and observe the you watching the black and white film of your phobic inducing interview incident

5. When the film reaches the end scene you are once again in a safe place after the interview has ended, pause the black and white film and turn it into a stilled black and white image

6. Leave the projection room and float back towards the you in the cinema seat, pass over yourself and step into the image of you in the cinema screen at the end of the phobic interview incident (in the safe place after the interview)

7. Change the picture to colour and ensure you are fully associated by seeing the world from the you in the film.

Run the film backwards like you would if you press rewind on a video player. Rewind the film so you see the interview running backwards; imagine you can see everyone moving backwards, even hear the voice of you and the interviewer in rewind. This should only take 1 or 2 seconds

8. Repeat this process several times until you can think of a job interview without feeling scared. If you feel any discomfort repeat the exercise 3-4 more times

9. While rewinding the film for a 3rd or 4th time add in step 2, 3 and 4 from destroying negative interview memories technique

With a new found confidence and a lack of nervous you are now ready to learn the secrets tricks for passing job interviews, whatever you do, DON'T share these secret interview tricks with everyone....

Commanding Confidence

1. If you imagine being confident, you will feel confident
2. In your mind, move negative images away and bring positive pictures forward
3. Challenge your limiting beliefs
4. Model confident people
5. Use your voice tone to empower your interview answers
6. Access your successful state before any job interview
7. Turn negative self talk into shapes and move the shape down your body
8. Play upbeat and fun music to negative memories

Sneaky Interviews Tricks:

Influential Rules 24 to 29

As a young child I was fascinated by magicians and all the tricks they could play; pulling rabbits out of hats, guessing your playing card that you randomly picked from a pack of 52 and chopping their beautiful assistants in two. After watching these shows I would try the tricks for myself, my parents didn't mind the card tricks but when I asked my dad to borrow his saw...Anyway, as an adult I am still intrigued by magicians, even though I know that everything I see is a trick or illusion of some sort and that magicians use psychology, misdirection and showmanship to confuse and delight their audiences I still appreciate the work they put in to pull what seems like an effortless trick.

It is the same with job interviews, the end result is to highlight our strengths and to be offered a job, and in similar ways to the magician we want to amaze our audience – the interviewers. We will use showmanship to gain rapport and to be seen as a confident person and we can also use psychology and persuasive techniques to increase our chances of job offers by ensuring the interviewer buys into you as a sound investment. And like the magician pulling a rabbit out of the hat or correctly guessing the Ace that you're holding, we want to deliver a good interview performance which means like the magician we need to practice, practice and practice these techniques.

Rule No.24 Destructive Nightmares

"It is never too late to be what you might have been."
— George Eliot

Getting a good night's sleep is key for any job interview as you need to feel alert and prepared for the interview questions. These 4 steps will help fall asleep instantly but you do need to start this technique in advance of the interview eve.

1. **Only use your bed for sleep, if you need to read, text, relax do it somewhere else as we want to associate tiredness to the bedroom**
2. **If you get into bed and you feel awake or when you wake up (often through brushing your teeth as this activity puts your body back into action which means you need to brush your teeth an hour before going to bed) get up and watch TV, read a book and return to bed only when you feel sleepy**
3. **Turn off your phone and don't listen to music, if needed wear sleep masks to create a dark atmosphere. If you're a tidy person and can't sleep unless the room is tidy, then tidy up long before you prepare to go to bed**
4. **Try and stick to a pattern by going to bed at a certain time each night, but the key here is to only get into bed when you're tired as this will create an anchor out of the bed – making you feel more sleepy as you climb into bed**

Association is key to falling asleep instantly, you can see association everywhere; sports stars will "wear their lucky jock strap" for a big game as they associate playing "a good game" with an item of clothing. Others will come home from work alert and instantly feel tired as they sit of their favourite seat, the seat that they sit on every night after work, even though only 3-4 seconds ago they were fully alert.

Many of you have heard of Pavlos's dog, Pavlov a Russian scientist was made famous by his discovery that he could control his dog's salivation by simply striking a bell. Each time he fed his dogs he would ring a bell which would cause the dogs to produce saliva to aid digestion of their food. The dog quickly associated the bell to feeding time and when Pavlov rang the bell even when there was no food, the dog would still salivate.

Having a great night's sleep will help you feel alive and alert on the morning of the interview. When heading off to the interview feeling confident after practising the confidence building exercise on a daily basis, you arrive and disaster – you have sweaty palms, will this result in leaving a bad first impression?"...

Rule No.25 Don't Let Your Handshake Show Your True Emotions

"I have not failed. I've just found 10,000 ways that won't work." — Thomas A. Edison

We all know that first impressions count during your interview. When being introduced to the interviewer, you will more often than not be committed to a handshake; a handshake is a quick gesture to say **"Hello I'm here, I'm professional and I'm ready for the interview"** this two second introduction will give the employer their first impression about you and sets the tone for the rest of the interview.

If you believe in the power of the handshake or not, your handshake is expected and often unconsciously tells the employer a little about your character, employers will often be prejudiced and make an opinion about you unconsciously from your initial handshake.

Research has shown that a handshake like other body language signals gives interviewers an unconscious idea about a person's personality and a firm handshake is more likely to help gain you a job offer, then a limp, damp handshake.

First, if you are nervous you will have sweaty hands, you don't need to keep wiping them dry, while you're in the waiting area as you will keep producing sweat until you start the interview and will subsequently end up with little bits of sweat soaked tissue all over your hands.

Which means you need to dry your hands as the interviewer is approaching you, to do this keep a tissue (kitchen roll is best) under your CV case/portfolio. This way the tissue is out of sight and when the interviewer approaches you, you can quickly wipe your hands dry underneath your folder, as the interviewer approaches you can give a firm and dry handshake portraying confidence rather than nerves.

With dry hands and a good first impression, you are now learning the hidden meanings of handshakes and what they secretly portray....

Rule No.26 Disarm the Interviewer with Your Handshake

"**Everything you can imagine is real.**" — Pablo Picasso

As we said, handshakes like all body language gives away how you are feeling — nervous or confident? And employers prefer to offer jobs to confident interviewees. Employers are not taught what a certain handshake represents but unconsciously your handshake and body language will give clues to the employer's subconscious mind.

- **If your Palm is facing up this can be taken as a sign of submission**
- **A palm facing down can be taken as aggressive**
- **A palm facing sideways is taken as a sign of equality**

If an interviewer uses the Palm Facing down handshake (aggressive) on you, you can counter this by putting your second hand on top of their hand and slowly turning their Palm up (this needs lots of practicing for it to look natural)

Employers will probably not remember the handshake itself, they remember the unconscious image they create of you from the handshake, just like our body language gives non verbal clues, and so does your handshake.

What makes a good handshake? **A firm grip, eye contact and an up-and-down movement.** Now you know what makes a good handshake, don't fall into the trap of stupidity and make a common handshake mistake:

- **The Bone Grinder** – don't turn a handshake into a competition to see who is the strongest.
- **The Extended Handshake** – a nervous interviewee will be pre-occupied with making a good impression and overcoming their nervous, that they will forget to let go of the interviewer's hand.
- **Slippery Eel** – again this one can often happen to nervous interviewees, the more nervous we become the more we sweat, remember to sneakily wipe your hands before the handshake.

Once you can give a fantastic first impression through a confident handshake you can back up your confidence, with your power voice to confirm your suitability.....

Rule No.27 The God Voice Technique

"What lies behind us and what lies before us are tiny matters compared to what lies within us." — Ralph Waldo Emerson

Are you a squeaker? Is your voice soft? Or are you just quiet? If you have answered yes to any of these questions or you just know your voice doesn't sound that confident, you will need to find your **God Voice**, so you can use this voice to influence the interview.

I recommend doing this exercise with a friend as you will both laugh and you we all learn more when were having fun.

- Find a big room, ideally a lecture hall or just stand in front of a big lake. First I want you to scream really loud, so loud that the people in the room above and the walker on the other side of the lake can hear you. Don't screech, scream - arrghhhhh!
- How did that feel? Good? It feels great screaming and letting it all out, so do it again ARRGHHHHHH!!!
- Next I want you to pretend that you are going to give a speech on all the activities that you took part in yesterday, from the moment you got up to the time you went to bed- make sure you don't miss anything out. Now imagine someone was at the back of the lecture hall (or send your friend there) or someone was on the other side of the lake and this person is a bit deaf.
- They are so deaf that you have to shout your story at them, word by word. Don't go quieter (or if you do tell your friend to shout "What did you say?") each word has to be as loud as the last, from the first word to the last.
- Notice that powerful feeling you feel inside when you use your power voice to shout? What does your power voice feel like? Where is this feeling inside? Where does this feeling originate from and where does this feeling spread to?

By doing this simple exercise you will first feel good and more importantly you have found your power voice, you can feel it in your stomach right now, if you shouted loud enough. Remember this power voice feeling, feel it again, now remember what it feels like, where the feeling is and how the powerful feeling spreads around your body.

Practice recalling this feeling so you can recollect the feeling of your power voice before your next interview. When attending your next interview you can you can use the feeling of your power voice; talk from the place your power voice comes from, to give you the confidence to talk louder but remember the interview isn't on the other side of a lake, so this time you can be a little quieter while still feeling the power voice inside you.

Before the interview, practice talking to friends and family using your power voice, talking from the place your power voice comes from and notice how different people react to you, await positive feedback and reactions – **"Wow you seem so much more confident!"**

A confident voice portrays honesty and believability; to further impress the employer you can answer questions quoting facts and figures, but as we see often on the "Dragons Den" remembering facts and figures isn't as easy as it seems, unless you use rule 28 – Master Memory Model....

Rule No.28 Master Memory Model

"If you don't like something, change it. If you can't change it, change your attitude. Don't complain." — Maya Angelou

Have you been in an interview and been asked a question, even a simple question like **"Where did you work previously?"** and your mind goes blank? What if you have to attend an interview where you need to quote large amounts of information like statistics, facts and figures or if you have to deliver a presentation without using a script?

The **Memory Palace** can help increase your memory capacity which will open up new possibilities for you. The Memory Palace is one of the most powerful memory techniques and what I like about it **is it is easy and fun to learn!** The Memory Palace technique is based on the fact that we remember the details of the places we know; our home, place of work or a local street - without having to think about it. By adding abstract images to these places with sounds and smells, you can store large amounts of information in these places (palaces as we will refer to them) that you can quickly access when needed.

Picking a Palace

First you need to pick your palace, your palace is a place you know well, this could be your house, your school, place of work or even a street you know well. You should be very familiar with the palace you choose, you need to be able to close your eyes and recall all of the details of the place or building.

When you imagine your palace, see it from your eyes as if you were there now, you need to feel fully associated with your palace, seeing what you can see, smelling the smells, hearing any sounds, tasting any taste and feeling the room's temperature or the touch of an objects you may brush pass, as if you were walking through your palace for real.

Close your eyes and in your mind's eye remember all the details of your palace as if you were there now.

Distinctive Features

As you walk through your palace start from the beginning, this may be a front door or the garden gate and notice all the details of your palace. If you can see a door notice the colour of the door, be aware if the paint is peeling off or just been newly coated, whatever the details are, become aware of them all now.

As you walk through your palace, in each room follow the same routine looking from left to right or right to left, as you visualise the room, be aware of any new taste or smells, make a mental note of anything that sticks out, anything that grabs your attention; a picture, a lamppost, an old chair.

If you struggle to remember parts of your palace either pick a new palace or physically go to your palace and walk through it for real. Continue to walk through your palace until you can easily remember all the details of every room.

Association

Take the list of items you want to remember and again visualise your memory palace from the beginning, we will call all the memory palace features that stuck out a **memory peg**.

Using a "memory peg" (a feature from your memory palace; example door, picture etc) combine it with the element you want to memorise – a statistic, interview answer; make this as crazy and unusual as possible, as our mind will quickly remember the unusual.

For each item you want to remember try to give it a visual reference, a sound, a taste, a smell and a feeling (internal or external) As an example, if a Personal Assistant wanted to remember a list of tasks she completed in a previous job and highlight her diverse range of skills during the job interview and she uses her own house as her memory palace, she would start by being stood outside her front door.

As she looks at her door, she might imagine a giant letter E coming through the letter box, getting bigger and bigger made out of the soft material you get in a car airbag. As it get so big it touches her face, she can feel the material on her face and she smells strongly the artificial man made smell of plastic and then, just as quick the giant E quickly deflates like a large balloon making a sound like someone passing wind. This represents her first task, checking her employer's, central and her own E-mail inboxes.

As she walks inside her palace past the front door, the next thing she sees is a lamp on a table (this is the actual lamp in her real house – peg), the lamp is turned on and sizzling on top of the lamp light bulb is a piece of bacon, as she inhales she can smell that lovely bacon smell. Tasting the bacon in her mouth, which will remind her of her second daily task; collecting breakfast for the senior corporate management team.

As you can tell, you can be as creative as you want using the memory palace technique. By using all of your senses; **visual, audio, feelings, taste and smells** your mind will be able to create a memorable memory. By placing random creative images throughout a room you know well, means you can remember information in a certain order making it easier to recall.

Re-Visit Your Palace

Repeat the journey a couple of times (especially if your new to this technique), starting from the same point each time, paying attention to all your memory pegs. Once you have finished, re-walk the route starting from the end (your last memory peg) and walking all the way back through your palace until you end at the beginning, seeing your visual images in reversed order.

Being asked questions on the content of your memory palace is always a great confidence boost, and from the employer's perspective they are impressed by the amount of information, facts and figures you can produce. As well as impressing people with your skilled memory you can impress employers with just your body.....

Rule No.29 Influence with Posture

"Life isn't about finding yourself. Life is about creating yourself." — George Bernard Shaw

You may have noticed that some of the key points you need to remember have been repeated throughout this book as repetition is the key to learning, and one of the key messages is how you can win over the interviewer by building rapport, highlighting your industry knowledge while selling your key selling points that match the employer's criteria.

To help build rapport and influence use your posture throughout the interview process – remember the subconscious is readings cues continually to give the conscious mind a true representation off you.

Entering the Interview Room.

After a 5 minute wait, the receptionist will ask you to enter the interview room; pick up your documents and take a deep breath, as you enter the interview room, walk straight in, the interviewer is expecting you (if the door is closed, knock first and then enter) don't just stand in the doorway. As you walk in, continue walking at the same speed towards the interviewer, an interviewee who is nervous will change their walking speed or will try to hide behind the door.

Meeting the Interviewer.

As you walk up to the interviewer, keep your eyes in the interviewer's general direction, don't stare. As you near the interviewer's desk, hold out your hand for the all important handshake. The interviewer, like most people will start to make an immediate impression about you, for this to be positive, smile as you shake hands (everyone likes a happy person and smiling has been proven to increase rapport) and introduce yourself using your **power voice.** In most cases the interviewer will ask for you to be seated, if they don't, sit down, a confident person will be used to taking control.

The Chair.

When seated, if you feel relaxed and calm, sit however you feel comfortable, if you feel comfortable you will come across well. Generally, sit forward a little and as the interviewer is talking nod your head, this shows agreement and builds rapport.

In most cases you will be sat opposite the interviewer, to show confidence turn your body 45 degrees so you are on a slight angle.

Feeling Nervous?

When you're nervous, your hands will tend to find a mind of their own and start pulling invisible loose cotton and/or start fidgeting. To stop this, link your fingers together, as it will take a conscious effort to pull them apart and to start fidgeting again.

Eye Contact.

You don't have to stare at the interviewer throughout the interview, actually don't stare at the interviewer throughout the interview, it would really put them off. As we think and remember past events from the interviewers questions, your eyes will naturally flicker all over the place, generally when giving your answer look at the interviewer, like you would when talking to a friend or family member. When in a panel interviewer, look from one interviewer to another when giving your answer.

To look confident, raise your chin slightly (practice this at home – it needs to look natural) people feeling nervous will keep their head down ("feeling down")

Preparing to Leave.

Be calm when preparing to leave, if you've brought any documents, take your time retrieving them, making small talk with the employer. Thank the interviewer for their time and shake the interviewer's hand. Like your entrance, walk out in a composed and confident manner; keep your head up and don't put your hands in your pocket.

The techniques throughout this book are already helping you prepare for your next job interview, but imagine you could mind reader the employer so you knew what they were thinking, if you could mind read the employer how would you use this skill to come across at your best during the job interview?....

Sneaky Interview Tricks

1. Associate sleep to your bed to ensure a good nights sleep
2. Dry your hands as the interviewer approaches
3. An equalling handshake portrays confidence
4. A strong interview applicant will have a power voice
5. Use the memory palace to remember large amounts of information
6. Confident body language will leave a lasting impression

Mind Read the Employer:

Influential Rules 30 to34

Can you really learn to mind read the interviewer? The idea of being able to mind read someone is something that has intrigued psychologist for years and the recent Derren Brown shows on TV has highlighted how powerful these techniques can be.

We can't look in to someone's eyes and know what that person is thinking in detail as we all think about thousands of different things all the time, we can't even process everything we sense in the world ourselves which is why we use filters; **deletions, distortions and generalisations**, which means if we want to mind read the employer we need to understand certain aspects of the person's character and how that person behaves in society, while picking up non verbal cues that all interviewers unconsciously gives away.

But before you learn to mind read, I want you to answer the following questions:

What is 5 + 1?

What is 4 + 2?

What is 2 + 4?

What is 1 + 5?

What is 3 + 3?

Say out loud, Blue, Orange, Black

What is the first vegetable you can think off?

Is it a carrot? With nine out of ten of you I would have guessed correctly as I have influenced your thoughts, the similar techniques throughout this book have been designed to help you influence your performance during the job interview and manipulate the interviewer.

Rule No.30 The Secret Power of Your Unconscious

"People always tell me with absolute certainty that they don't trust themselves" – Richard Bandler

Cold reading (reading none verbal cues) isn't new, as psychics have been reading people for years, picking up on non verbal cues and feeding back information the person has said to build rapport, trust and authenticity. This same technique used during a job interview can be highly powerful creating strong bond and for interview manipulation.

1. **First when mind reading, trust your intuition as your subconscious mind picks up more unconscious communication then you would believe. When mind readings don't think logically instead go with your "gut feeling." You may not know exactly what the person is thinking in terms of individual words (you will in various cases as people have automatic responses to certain words or situations depending on their experiences and personality) but you will know whether the person is about to say something positive or negative and I would add in an interview situation having this knowledge is a big advantage as I will also be teaching you soon how to use language patterns to influence the interview**

2. **Pupil Sizes - watch for changing of pupil size to know if someone is interested in you or what you have to say, as shrinking pupils generally mean the person is not interested, while enlarging pupils is a sign of interest**

3. **Watch hand movements – when people talk they give away clues with their hand movements. In panel interviews the employer may say something along the lines of "I can see you would fit in well with my team, but there could be one or two obstacles to overcome.." While pointing at a colleague, unconsciously he is saying you need to persuade**

this one. People describe how they feel unconsciously with hand movements, we have all heard "I've had it up to here" while seeing someone gesture a level (where they have had it up to) by moving their flattened hand up to their forehead.

4. When giving an interview answer that requires a large amount of communication watch out for the interviewer tapping their feet or drumming their figures – this is a sign that they want to get away. In this instance you have two choices – 1. Create intrigue to encourage the interviewer to be interested in you again or 2. Summarise and quickly move on!

5. Interviewers will nod when they unconsciously agree with you; this is highly reassuring when you're explaining your strengths or ideas. When in rapport you will also notice the interviewer mirror your body posture and may even mirror your blinking and breathing rhythm

6. You may ask the interviewer "do you inspire creativity from your employees?" as an example interview question, the interviewer may respond "yes" while touching their nose unconsciously this can highlight that they are lying (or don't truly believe their own answer)

* when reading body language it is best to look for clusters of body language and gestures before creating an opinion as one single clue can be easily misinterpreted as an interviewer may scratch their nose (which could be taken as a cue that the interviewer is lying) because they had an itchy nose.

These 5 introductory steps to mind reading will help you understand how to pick up cues from people's body language and gestures by trusting your instincts. You will now learn more in-depth techniques to understanding your interviewers mind, but like all of the techniques you need to practice reading these cues and unconsciously know what they mean. To do this go to parties and public places when you see people in rapport or flirting - use this opportunities to observe and become aware of their body language, how far apart they stand, if they touch each other and the direction of their feet.

Observe people who are not getting on or are talking to each other to be polite, again be aware of their body language and gestures; are they tapping their foot, what direction are their feet facing, do they look away often or drink more of their drinks, are they talking while making gestures with their hands or do they have their hands in their pockets?

You will quickly become an expert of reading cues the more you practice cue reading by observing people.

To help you in your quest to read people, you will now find a list of common body signals that you can easily interpret; we have picked body signals that you will see used in job interviews and the more you can read body language the more you will be able to mind read the employer...

Rule No.31 Read the Interviewer Like a Book

"A creative man is motivated by the desire to achieve, not by the desire to beat others" - Ayn Rand

Being able to read body language accurately can give you a large advantage over other interviewees as a person able to read body language will know when their interview answer is going well, keeping the interviewer interested in you or when you are starting to bore or annoy the interviewer.

We will cover the basics in this book but I would highly recommend reading a specialist body language book and I would add, a specialist book will tell you the importance of recognising a number of body language cues in cluster rather than isolated incidents in order to be able to interpret them correctly.

It is also good to note that some body language signals differ depending on the person's culture, so we have covered some of the universal body language signals here.

The Shoulder Shrug when discussing a situation and a person shrugs their shoulders; this can mean that the person does not understand what you mean. In an interview situation you will need to re-word what you have said or express your answer in a different way

Crossed Arms Across the Body many of us heard that crossed arms means the person is putting up a barrier. This is a defensive piece of body language showing you the person disagrees with you or they don't like what you are saying

Touching Lips when telling lies our unconscious mind automatically sends a signal to our hands to cover our mouth to stop the deceitful words from escaping, which is why when people touch their lips when talking it can often be taken for a sign that the person is lying – remember though look for clusters not just a one expression

Open Palms when people show their palms, this is an "open" gesture showing that the person is being honest and open

Playing with Cuffs people playing with their cufflinks or picking an invisible piece of cotton on their shirt will do this by crossing their arm across their chest which you have already learnt is a barrier. People will play with cufflinks when they feel nervous, uncomfortable or tense

Hand Clench people clench their hands together (fingers interlocked) when they feel frustrated, don't be tricked if the interviewer with clenched hands is smiling as deep down they will still feel frustrated

Hand Supporting Head if you observe an interviewer resting their head on their hand (normally with a finger pointing upwards) is a sign that the interviewer is having negative thoughts about you or what you are saying

The Catapult the catapult shape is created when a person leads back and puts both arms behind their head with their elbows pointing outwards, people do this when they feel confident, dominant, superior or is a "know it all"

When I first learnt to read body language I would watch other people, check their posture and refer to my body language book, but I also became distinctly aware of my own body language as I displayed all of these body language behaviours as I was cocky, bored, flirtatious, annoyed, in control or restless. As well as reading body language you can learn to read eye pattern cues, as the old saying goes "the eyes are the windows to your soul"....

Rule No.32 Look Away and Miss the Hidden Clues the Eyes Give Away

"Always desire to learn something useful" - Sophocles

The eyes are the windows to your soul; being able to notice a person's eye direction movements and to recognise what they mean will provide you with some essential information about how interviewers are processing/thinking information.

Eye movements indicate how a person is thinking - whether they are imagining a future or past event, internally re-hearing a voice or creating a sound, talking to themselves, or accessing their emotions.

When explaining information or listening to your answers the interviewer will be processing what you are saying, from your point of view <u>you need to know how they are processing the information</u> so you know how to influence the interviewer.

So, let's say, you are **explaining** to an interviewer how you would do X and they say they do not understand - <u>while looking UP to either</u>

the left or the right (indicating that they may be visualising or trying to visualise). This could indicate to you that the interviewer needs you to **demonstrate,** rather than verbally explain, so they will be able to **see** how to do it.

This chart highlights the eye movement and how the brain processes information (eye accessing cues as seen if you are facing the interviewer)

- Beware that some people (often left handed people) will use eye cues in the opposite direction

To quickly become an expert at reading eye cues, ask a friend to sit opposite you and ask them these following questions, don't listen to their answer but notice their eye movements and match them to the chart above.

Looking Up and to the right-Visual Remembered
- What is the colour of the shirt you wore yesterday?
- Which of your friends has the shortest hair?

Looking up and to the left-Visual Constructed
- What would your room look like if it were painted yellow with big purple circles?
- Can you imagine the top half of a tiger on the bottom half of an elephant?

Looking to the Right (towards ears) -Auditory Remembered
- What does your best friend's voice sound like?

- Which is louder, your door bell or your telephone?

Looking to the Left (towards ears) - Auditory Constructed
- What will your voice sound like in 10 years?
- What would it sound like if you played your two favourite pieces of music at the same time?

Looking down to the Right - Auditory Internal
- What is something you continually tell yourself?
- What are your thoughts about this book?

Looking Down to the Left-Kinaesthetic
- What does it feel like to walk barefoot on a warm sandy beach?
- What does it feel like when you rub your fingers on sandpaper?

When an interviewer is talking their eyes will be flickering to reflect where they are processing what they are saying internally. As an example the interviewer may say **"We want this project to be a success.."** while looking up and to the left (visual constructed) so we know they have an vision of how they want this project to go, they have imagined the project's success. If the employer looked up and to the right (visual remembered) they may want the project to be as successful as a past (remembered) project, which allows you ask question on this past project rather than offering just your ideas.

When asking an interviewer a question, say on how you would fit in with their team and they look down and left (kinaesthetic) before looking back at you, you now they know they accessed their emotions to feel if you would fit rather than visualising you fitting in.

By noticing the interviewers eye movements you can become more aware of how they are thinking and processing your answers. Some interviewers will have strong preferences to one of the three ways we process information **(Visual, Auditory or Kinaesthetic),** as an example musicians often have a stronger preference to their auditory senses as they use this section of their brain on a more regular basis.

When an interviewer has a strong preference to one of their senses they will unconsciously give this way with the language patterns they use, once you can pick up their language pattern, you can use THEIR words to communicate more effectively....

Rule No.33 Use Distracting Words at Your Peril

"Language is the blood of the soul into which thoughts run and out of which they grow" - Oliver Wendell Holmes

To communicate effectively we need to use the words the interviewer uses to increase rapport and to influence on a higher level of scale. We all see, hear and feel the world around us in a different way and our version of the world is leaked through our language. If you are talking to a Visual person with kinaesthetic language they often won't often be able to appreciate fully what you are trying to get across to them.

- Visual people will often use words like; **Birds-Eye View, Focus, Glance, Take a dim view, Mind's eye, Vision, Imagine, Examine, Expose, Graphic, Outlook, Vague.**

Visual people will often look up as they talk (Visualising pictures in their mind)

- Auditory people will often use words like; **Clear as a Bell, Outspoken, Word for Word, Mention, Manner of Speaking, Loud and Clear, Report, Say, Shout, Sing, Silence.**

Auditory people will often look to the side when talking (towards their ears)

- Kinaesthetic people will often use words like; **Affected, Feel, Heat, Cold, Emotional, Touch, Tickle, Tap, Heated, Handle, Hot-headed, Tied, Irritate, Get a Load of This.**

Kinaesthetic people will often look down when talking (towards their feelings; stomach – "I have a gut feeling")

How can this help? By knowing someone's primary representational system, you can use this when communicating with them. This enhances communication as you are **"speaking their language"** and increases rapport.

Like we said before if someone **feels** you're like them, they will like you. If you use the interviewer's representational system preferences when answering questions, the interviewer will understand exactly what you are trying to get across to them.

Have you ever tried to get a point over to someone and they just don't understand no matter how much you repeat yourself? In most cases this happens when two people with different representational preferences are having a conversation. If you used different **wording** to match their representational preference it would have made a big difference.

How would you respond to this statement?

"I **see**, but I'm not **visualising** these new **ideas** of yours"- Visual Person

- "I can give you a **clear picture** by **showing** you this **illustration**"
- "You will **feel** different once you're given the **hard** evidence and you will be able to **get to grips with it**"
- "Once you **hear** the results **word for word**, it will be **clear as a bell**"

Practice this technique on friends and family before you go to an interview; the more you practice the more natural it will become, also watch how people react differently to your conversation changes. This really works and is so easy to learn.

When talking the interviewers' language you will meet one of the rules of psychology - that people naturally like people who are like them, to enhance this, you can increase likeability through commonality....

Rule No.34 Build Likeability through Commonality

"If you can dream it, you can do it" - Walt Disney

People like people who are like them, if you can get the interviewer to instantly like you, you will automatically build rapport increasing your changes of a job offer. These 5 tips will help you build likability through commonality.

1. **Everyone has something in common with another person, the key is to find out what this is and use it as an icebreaker. This shows that you are interested in the person not just the job offer. Remember, we like to say yes to people we like**

2. **To build rapport, listen intently when the interviewer is talking, reassuring through positive body language and head nodding, that you are interested.**

3. **Don't interrupt and always ask questions, this indicates that you are interested, if they feel safe and they like you they will keep the conversation flowing.**

4. **Mirroring body language can be equalising – When talking to someone who is sat down you should also sit. By sitting down (or standing up if required!) you ensure your eye line is level with the other person. You are establishing yourself as an equal rather than an aggressive or submissive individual.**

5. **Don't paraphrase, parrot-phrase! When asking questions or providing answers, use the words the interviewer used,**

as people create pictures in their mind from the words you use, which means <u>different words create different pictures</u>, as we all see the world differently — remember the mini exercise? By parroting the interviewer you will reinforce the interviewer's image of you rather then confusing the image in the employers mind by adding your own slant to it.

You already understand how easy is it to read people, we have looked at gestures and talked about language cues, which means you are getting a good grasp on the basics of influencing and persuasion techniques and I would add a key to influencing interviews is by understanding the interviewers' personality type and then using this to manipulate them...

Mind Read the Employer

1. Look for clusters of body language to make an informed 'mind reading' opinion
2. Master positive and negative body postures
3. Use eye cues to understand how the interviewer is processing information
4. Reply using the interviewers language patterns to deepen rapport
5. Share commonality to increase likeability

Persuasion through Personality:

Influential Rules 35 to39

To really understand your interviewer and then persuade them, you need to quickly gain an insight into a person's personality, which is easier to learn then you may think.

Our personality is broken down into **4 main sections** and each section has a choice of 2 personality preferences; where we get our energy from **(extrovert or introvert)** how we take in information **(sensing or intuition)** how we make decisions **(feeler or thinker)** and your attitude to life **(judger or perceiver)**

By understanding each section and personality type choice, you can understand your interviewer's personality and mind, with this insight you can change your language to influence and persuade the interviewer to, well offer you a job. A person's personality type reflects their values, attitudes and perceptions which is why understanding your employer's mind can <u>make a real difference</u> in how you can influence the interview.

It is good to understand that we all possess both types of each of the 4 personality sections, but people generally have a strong preference to one of each of the 4 personality sections.

Rule No.35 Energise the Interviewer

"The key is to keep company only with people who uplift you, whose presence calls forth your best" - Epictetus

The first section of a person's personality type is often easy to spot, as you start to understand extroversion and introversion in more detail you quickly recognise people with this trait.

Extrovert people get their energy from the outside world, they like to be around others and are good talkers, people on the high end on the extrovert scale will constantly interrupt you as they have an urge to say what they are thinking and they usually do.

An extrovert interviewee is the type of person to open up a conversation in the waiting area, the type of person at home who shouts at the TV. Extrovert people are quick to respond to situations, in an interview situation if your interviewer has a strong extrovert preference you may find that you struggle to get a word in, as the interviewer will ask the question and may even answer it for you.

How to notice an extrovert

- **They talk quickly and say what is on their mind**
- **Their sentences last longer than other peoples**
- **They may interrupt you even when they have asked you a question**
- **They are loud and animated**
- **They will often use lots hand gestures and facial expressions**

Introverted people get their energy from going inside themselves; they like quiet and are often seen as a good listener. Introvert people will talk and join in with others but are keener to think about what they are going to say rather than just saying it.

Introvert people concentrate on the task at hand; they don't need others to motivate them as they work best in solitary. The introvert person is the person who will turn off the TV, radio and their phone when they need to study or concentrate on a task. An introvert interviewer may pause after you have answered a question to digest this new information and to prepare their next statement or question.

How to notice an introvert

- **They will listen more then they will talk**
- **They will think before they act**
- **They will often keep their thoughts to themselves until they feel ready to share their insights**
- **They will speak slowly and carefully and their speech can be quiet in volume**
- **They rarely use non-verbal communication such as gestures**

One section of the personality trait that you want to master, is the interviewers decision making process, if you can master influencing this section of the interviewers personality, you can at very less make they want you, at the extreme you can basically get the employer to offer you a job...

Rule No.36 Influence the Interviewers Decision Making Process

"In any moment of decision the best thing you can do is the right thing, the next best thing is the wrong thing, and the worst thing you can do is nothing" - Theodore Roosevelt

We decide or come to conclusions through our personal values and our emotions (how we feel about a certain choice) or through logical reasoning and intellectual processing.

A feeling person is highly in contact with their emotions, they are highly sensitive which leads them to not wanting to give out criticism or receive it. Feelers will decide by literally thinking about <u>how they feel</u> about the situation – does it feel good or bad?

You can spot a Feeler by

- **They need to be liked by others, they will often agree with what the majority say is right and don't like saying no to people**
- **They will seek out others to see if their OK, an interviewer with a "feeling" preference may ask you "Do you have everything you need?" "Are you feeling comfortable, do you want me to open a window.."**
- **They are affected by the atmosphere and driven my emotion**
- **They are highly aware of their values and accommodate others until their values have been violated and then they will turn on you**
- **They appear warm and friendly and are diplomatic and tactful**

A person with a thinker personality is driven mainly by reason and logic; all decisions are made in their "head" rather than with emotions. A thinker can be friendly but is more detached to their feelings which means the thinker may tell you have made a mistake in a straight forward (**"You did A, B and C which was wrong."**), wanting to help you, but their communication may be interpreted by others as blunt and too quick to the point.

You can often spot a Thinker as:

- **They may argue or debate facts (for fun) as they like to hear both sides of an argument**
- **They can make tough decisions without becoming emotionally attached**
- **They like rules and principles and will follow them**
- **They are honest, direct and take few things personally**
- **They can be impatient when others are emotional**

Throughout this book, one of the ongoing topics is to ensure your key selling point is filtered through to the interviewer throughout the interview, creating a powerful image of you that the employer will desire, without the interviewer generalising or distorting what you have said. You can do this through matching language and reading the employers body language cues. Next you need the employer to pay attention and to digest fully the information you present....

Rule No.37 Disguise the Information You Give the Employer

"Lack of direction, not lack of time, is the problem. We all have twenty-four hour days" — Zig Ziglar

We pay attention, take in information, notice the outside world and remember facts in two distinct different ways. A sensor will notice all the facts and details of a situation, while an intuitive person will focus more on the bigger picture and possibilities.

Sensing people are practical and literal, they tend to stick to that they know will work – they may take the same route to work each day. A sensing person is interested in detail, they like to know the facts and admire practical solutions.

You can notice sensing people by

- **They work at a steady pace and live in the here and now**
- **They work best from step-by-step instructions**
- **They will use straight forward and simple language**
- **They prefer to test things out for buying into it**
- **There observant and are good at remembering information**

Intuitive people like to focus and *what it could be* – they like to look at the possibilities of an idea. They will often trust their gut instinct and admire creative ideas. An intuitive person will skim through your CV, rather than read the CV in full to make an overall impression of you. Intuitive people like to figure things out for themselves, relying on their imagination and can work on many jobs at any one time.

Intuitive people have the following traits:

- **They use vague language and can be spontaneous**
- **They like variety and new experiences   -   they will often notice something new or different**
- **They enjoy learning new skills and hate routine**
- **They will often misplace or lose things and can miss important information**
- **They will take an idea and add to it, sometimes making big changes so the end product is nothing like the original idea**

Interviews are stressful for both the interviewee and the interviewer. The interviewer is ready to invest in a new employee, which means a wrong choice can cost companies thousands of pounds. Knowing that you can add value to the organisation is not enough, you need to ensure the employer understands what it is exactly that you will bring to the organisation...

Rule No.38 Deliver Your Answers the Way They Will Be Best Understood

"Failing to plan is planning to fail" - Alan Lakein

A certain environment can make one person stressed while another person within the same environment may feel at home and at ease. A judger prefers a structured environment where there is order, neatness and organisation. While a perceiver will *go with the flow* they can work in a mess and are happy to do things last minute as they like to keep their options open.

A judger likes to have things settled; they like to feel in control and take responsibility seriously and feel comfortable in management roles. Judgers will plan and think ahead, in an interview situation they will have a list of questions that will be asked in a certain order. Once a judger has made a decision they find it hard to change their mind.

You can see judger by

- **They pay attention to time and are usually on time, as they find comfort in schedules**
- **They will have a clean desk with everything in neat piles. There folders will be organised and colour coded with a contents page**
- **They will use diaries and to-do list; they will gain satisfaction from ticking list items of their list as they are completed**
- **They will prefer to start and complete a task before starting the next assignment**
- **They tend to be efficient and hate last minute surprises**

A perceiver hates to feel tied down, as they like to work in a flexible way. They can easily change their mind after they have made a decision and they are energised when they are working close to deadlines. A perceiver works often in a messy environment and they generally like to play first and work later.
A perceiver can be spotted by

- **They are playful and casual people who feel spontaneous**
- **They can juggle properties and do tasks at the last minute – they may come across as chaotic**
- **They will search for new experiences and will try to attempt the impossible**
- **They prefer to start tasks but don't always finish them. They might write lists but will often lose them**
- **They like plans to be flexible and can find it hard making a decision**

Having all the ingredients won't make a perfect dish, you first need to know what goes together and in what order. You have learnt the types to people's personalities, now you can learn to put these types together to influence and persuade through personality...

Rule No.39 Persuade Through Personality

"One of the best ways to persuade others is with your ears by listening to them" - Dean Rusk

As you can see by breaking down a person's personality into the 4 personality sections it is easy to work out a person's personality traits and once you can quickly pickup on an interviewers personality traits you use this information to persuade and influence them.

To persuade your interviewer you have to influence their decision making process and as you have already learnt, people make decisions through **Feeling or Thinking** and these decisions are taken in by the information we receive through our **Senses or Intuition.**

You will have a strong preference to F, T, S, N (N = intuition) and one of these will be more dominant then the other (F or T and S or N) and will be accompanied by the other personality trait.

So, the 4 possible persuasion types for persuasion are:

- **ST – Sensing and Thinker**
- **SF – Sensing and Feeler**
- **NF – Intuition and Feeler**
- **NT – Intuition and Thinker**

People like people who are like themselves, as you talk and act using the interviewer's natural personality preference they will naturally have a liking to you. But more importantly by presenting information in the way the interviewer best processes that information you will know your interview answers are hitting the mark. **To Influence an:**

ST – Sensing and Thinker; Be objective, realistic and logical

- Focus on specifics and facts
- Show how your ideas will work, indicating how it will save money and time
- Give specifics – dates, percentages, numbers, applications and benefits
- Talk about the "now" and how you can benefit the company today
- Explain things logically

SF – Sensing and Feeler; be practical, carful and helpful

- Use personal language and look for shared interest and values
- Show respect and listen carefully while using positive body language
- Give detail – dates, numbers and figures
- Show how your answer benefits the interviewer and the company
- State your benefits, don't just imply them

NF – Intuition and Feeler; be enthusiastic, creative and loyal

- Highlight the big idea for their organisation
- Point out how you will help people grow and develop
- Ask lots of questions and then listen intently
- Go with the flow when the interviewer digresses
- Explain what new things you can bring to the role

NT – Intuition and Thinker; be creative, strategic and rational

- Search by asking probing questions for the interviewer's ideas at the onset of the interview - show you recognise their vision
- Answer and address any difficult questions
- Highlight your ideas, broad and far reaching possibilities, emphasising uniqueness
- Give options but be logical in your proposals

- **Discuss the theory and background of your answer**

Now you know how to persuade the interviews information taking and decision making process you can now look at the final two personality sections and the 4 separate personality traits (E or I and P or J) remember people like people who are like them so if your interviewer is an E, I, P or J you can build rapport quickly by matching their personality.

E – Extrovert

- **Be energetic and full of life**
- **Listen when the interviewer talks and be prepared to be interrupted**
- **Turn the question and answer session into a conversation**
- **Use gestures and body language**
- **Repeat your main points**

I – Introvert

- **Give the interviewer time to absorb your answers – don't be tempted to fill gaps unless the gaps come from you not having an answer to a question**
- **Don't let your answers go on for too long**
- **Speak slowly so you are understood**
- **Don't move about on a squeaky chair as I's don't like interruptions**
- **Say to the interviewer "think about how we can implement X.." get them to go into themselves to think about you in a positive way**

J – Judger

- **Start and finish your answer – be concise, don't be tempted to mention a skill or experience that is not relevant to the current question**

- Explain how you complete tasks in time and that you don't like leaving things to the last minute
- Highlight the usefulness of diaries and list
- Give structured answers
- Explain how you quickly come to decisions which results in the task being completed competently

P – Perceiver

- Explain that you can go with the flow and when needed you can drop a task to meet a new priority before returning to the old task
- Highlight your ability to juggle a number of tasks at any one time
- Give an answer with several options – let the interviewer choose which one will fit
- When answering situation questions, discuss and go beyond the original question
- Talk about how you will bring a new experience to the organisation

A great way to understand your employer's personality is in the initial interview questions that are designed to get you to feel relaxed. The interview has already started before you take your seat, on the walk to the interview room, this opportunity can easily be used as an opportunity to informally find common ground, an opportunity not to be missed!

Think back to a past time when you were on a date, especially the dates that went really well – what happened? In most cases you would have asked lots of probing questions without being too personal, you would've listened intently when the other person was talking and you would have found common ground **"They're my favourite band too.."**

These 3 simple steps: **1. Asking questions, 2. Listening and 3. Finding common ground** leads to instant rapport between you and your interviewer and what does strong rapport result in? A second date or in this case, a job offer.

As well as building rapport, use these initial questions to work out the interviewer's personality; if they talk a lot they maybe an **Extrovert**, if they veered over to the quieter side then they may be an **Introvert**. Someone who gives creative ideas maybe **Intuitive** while someone stating details and facts maybe a **Sensor**. For an interviewer who tells it like it is may be a **Thinker** while the interviewer who is in touch with their emotions may be a **Feeler**. And for someone with a preference for order maybe a **Judger** and for someone who will talk about several topics in one go may be a **Perceiver**.

To be confident of accuracy when reading a person's personality, you need to find patterns of personalities, as we all have and use the 8 elements in our personality spectrum but we have a strong preference to 4 of the 8 personality elements. With this in-depth knowledge of control that you are building up you will already be one step ahead of the other interviewees, you can now prepare for answering those tricky interview questions...

Persuasion Through Personality

1. Extrovert people are loud and chatty, while Introvert are quiet and thoughtful
2. A feeler makes decisions based on their emotions, Thinkers makes decisions based on logic
3. Sensing people will notice the facts and details of a situation, where as a Intuitive person will focus on the bigger picture and possibilities
4. A Judger works best with order and organisation and a Perceiver is more happy going with the flow

---

Interview Questions and Presentations:

Influential Rules 40 to 47

Several years ago, I was attending a job interview; I had completed all the necessary research and prepared fully for my interview. While waiting in the reception area I saw a sign behind the receptionist desk saying *"Company Name"* and then stated two separate years which I quickly worked out to be a gap of 25 years – I had quickly armed myself with an additional snippet of information.

"So, what do you know about our company?" interviewer asked as his opening question.

"Well you have been established for around 25 years..." I answered confidently, but a confused response ensued.

"25 years? No, we have been established for 45 years, the business was established by my father...but we have been in this building for 25 years, we had a big celebration earlier this month and I presented a plaque that we have up in reception.."

Don't fall into the trap I did, to win job interviews you have to be fully prepared. You can learn to predict the interview questions as well as mastering the art of delivering killer answers that will blow the competition away.

Rule No.40 Predict The Interview Questions

"Things do not happen. Things are made to happen"
- John F. Kennedy

An excellent way to predict interview question is to ask the interviewers! By becoming an industry expert, as we discussed earlier on you will already have a good idea of the potential interview questions, won't you? As interviewers will only ask questions on the job role (duties) and the skills and qualities required for this position.

We have already looked at predicting potential interview questions from the job specification; this is one exercise that you should return to before your next job interview. The job specification is the interviewer telling you what they require from you which means the questions you will be asked will be based on these essential criterions.

By being able to predict the interview questions you can prepare your interview answers, but don't practice too much as you want your answer to sound natural and unrehearsed. There is no better feeling during a job interview then when the interviewer asks you a question that you know you have an excellent planned answer to. When this happens take your time and say **"That's a good question.."** while looking up creating an impression that you didn't expect them to ask questions along those lines, this will make your answer sound even more impressive.

But, why make work for yourself? We know we can predict interview questions, but why predict the questions, when there is a chance that your prediction is wide of the mark? Why not, just ask industry experts for the questions and more importantly the answers....

Rule No.41 Get The Experts To Give You The Answers

"What you get by achieving your goals is not as important as what you become by achieving your goals"
- Henry David Thoreau

Before your interview, ideally when you're at the job searching stage join several industry forums under an alias, add an introduction about yourself and join some forum discussions as this will show some commitment to the forum.

Once you have made a few comments (we do this so more people answer your future questions) start a new thread and use a catchy title to catch the attention of more people, which will increase the amount of people who will be likely to answer your question – something along the lines of **"5 embarrassing ways I messed up a job interview"**.

Explain that you have an interview coming up and give a quick explanation of how you embarrassing messed up your last job interview (this is why you used an alias – you never know your future boss could be on the same industry forum) and ask for sample interview questions and answers for your job industry.

You now have a list of industry interviews questions and potential answers that you can tailor to your own experience. Most of these questions will be the questions that future colleagues were asked themselves, during their job interview, which is why you have used an industry forum. You may fall lucky and get an industry interviewer offering you advice.

You can get questions from industry employees but each employer requires a different set of skills, which is why you need to re-read the job specification to match the expert's answers to your job interview. Alternatively Google *"interview questions and* answers" and you should find a range of possible interview answers you can fit to your own experience. In some ways this research stage is like being a website detective...

Rule No.42 Become a Website Detective

"What you do today can improve all your tomorrows"
- Ralph Marston

One final piece of research you need to undertake is as a website detective. All companies possess a website, with many companies having a "History" or "About us" tab. With many companies they will record their company values and mission statement and as you did when you matched the interviewers personality, to the way you structured your interview questions to build rapport and to influence them, you can match your values and career mission to that of the company's.

It is very easy to quickly understand what the key values are for most companies from their website, as you will find their values are mentioned several times on each of the website pages. When this happens be sure to <u>highlight how this value is important to you</u> and when possible give an example of when you have met this value in past positions.

With many companies they will have their values and/or mission recorded under "Our Mission" "Our Values" which makes things really easy for us. As an example our mission at Employment King is **to help people have the best possible Life, Career and Future by giving you the tools and techniques to support yourself.** So, for those of you reading this book to use the techniques to secure a job with Employment King, you would need to show your commitment to helping people as this is the core of the organisation.

If you can't find the company values or mission go back to the industry forums and social network sites and ask the experts, once you know what is important to this particular organisation, you can learn how to structure your interview answers in such away, for them to make a real impact....

Rule No.43 Structuring Your Interview Answers Will Increase the Acceptability of the Interviewer

"When you fail you learn from the mistakes you made and it motivates you to work even harder" - Natalie Gulbis

OK I'm not going to write a list of interview questions and answers here, if you want a FREE copy of **"Tricky Questions and Killer Answers – Over 60 interview questions and answers"** add this url: http://www.employmentking.co.uk/interviews/tricky-questions-killer-answers-e-book/ to your browser and enter the code **tkqa299**

The key to passing job interviews is **Communication**, the employer needs to understand what you are trying to communicate to them; communication is not about what you are saying, it's about how the other person interprets what you are saying which means you need to structure your interview answer in such a way that employer has no doubt you can do the specific part of the job that the interview question related to.

You may be asked **direct interview questions**; what, where, why, who or **competency based questions**; give me an example, describe a time when you, summarise your previous role and duties.

It's not about the type of question you are asked it's about how you structure your answer, which means you need to know how to plan and answer interview questions. I would add you need your answer to come across loud and clear by delivering up to **3 key pieces of information per answer**, any more then this can confuse the interviewers mind, as the brain can find it hard to consciously remember a large amount of information in one go.

The structure of the interview answer can be broken down into 3 stages: **1. Answer the question in the first sentence, 2. Add detail and intrigue and 3. Summarise your interview answer.**

1. **Start by answering the interview question in the first sentence**

Q: Are you a good team player?

A: Yes <u>I am a good team player</u>, in my last position I worked in team environment throughout entirety of the project...

Q: What is your knowledge of diversity and equal opportunities regulations?

A: <u>I possess a deep understanding of diversity and equal opportunity regulations</u>; I find it really important to keep up to date with changes to regulations...

Q: Where do you see yourself in 5 years time?

A: I am really <u>keen to turn this position into a career, in 5 years time</u> I will have a full understanding of the job sector and will be applying for a promotion within this organisation.

Q: Describe a situation where you dealt with an angry customer.

A: In my last position I would work on the complaints department <u>every Monday and would often come across angry customers</u> who had issues that needed resolving; I was always able to quickly calm customers down and resolve their issues by...

2. **Next add a little more detail – this should intrigue the employer and hit several of the job specifications essential criteria**

- Give an overview of the situation – In many cases this is done when you answer the question in your first sentence.
- Explain any "problems" or "barriers" you had to face and overcome **"The company had never had a contract like this**

before" "sales had started to drop, so the manger asked me to join the team.."
- Explain what YOU did "I **was responsible for..**" "I took **initiative..**" "**It was my idea to...**"
- Explain the positive outcome from your actions; where possible quote figures and percentages or give a third person feedback **"This led to an increase in sales by 35%" "The team manager fed back that this resulted in an increase in company shares"**

   3. **Finally, summarise by referring back to the question (this can also come across as you thinking of your answer on the spot, not using a prepared answer)**

- "Does that example highlight the team player skills you are looking for?"
- "I have a wide range of knowledge of diversity and equal opportunity regulations, would you like me to quote anymore?"
- "Overall I am happy to stay in this company and work my way up the career ladder"
- "To summarise I have come across a wide range of angry customers, but once you know how to calm and resolve their issues, you generally increase your customer retention"

As you can see from the 4 examples above, some of the summaries end with a question; this is a great additional trick to check if you have hit the interviewers required points to their question. If you have covered everything you will hear a reply like **"Yes that was a nice answer"** or **"I think we have covered everything"** if you haven't you will often be told **"I was looking for an example when you X"** you can then give a new example covering X or the interviewer may ask you a second but more specific question, it is good to be asked a second question so you can give the answer the employer requires, if not you will be forgotten, which means no job offers.

Using the job specification, your industry research and the questions from your free e-book **Tricky Questions, Killer Answers** - you have now a list of planned questions and perfected answers, that start by

117

answering the question in the first sentence, following by a more detailed answer and ending with a summary relating back to the initial question and like an actor remembering their lines, their posture and stage direction the more they practice, the more polished performance they deliver....

Rule No.44 Repetition Increase's Skill

"You can never quit. Winners never quit, and quitters never win"- Ted Turner

As with learning any new skill, practice makes perfect and passing job interviews on a regular basis is a skill you can learn. The best learners are often babies because they have an instinct to learn, because to learn is to survive, you can learn too, as a younger you, you learnt to walk, you learnt to talk and you learnt to read. You learnt so many things in your life that you should <u>feel inspired to learn more.</u> You learnt to cook, to drive, you learnt your job duties, you learnt to tie your shoelaces, and you learnt to make love, how many other things have you learnt?

With any learning, from learning to walk to learning to juggle, we all go through four stages from unconscious incompetency and unconscious competency.

- **Unconsciously Incompetent**
- **Consciously Incompetent**
- **Consciously Competent**
- **Unconsciously Competent**

Before attending your first interview you are **unconsciously incompetent** basically you don't know that you are nervous or incompetent during job interviews, until you attend the interview. It's the same as a baby not knowing it can't walk; the baby sees people walking and gives it a go, as it falls over it realises it can't walk. And then you become **consciously incompetent** – this experience has taught you that you are incompetent at that particular task.

As you read interview books, practice techniques, learn from your mistakes, prepare interview answers you <u>become more competent</u> during the job interview. As you learn from your interview feedback and practice through real or fake interviews you become **consciously competent** you are now competent at job interviews but this is conscious for many we have to try hard to be competent at interviews, just as the baby walking with her hands out just in case she falls, she can walk but has to make a conscious effort to balance and walk well. From this stage you will quickly become **unconsciously competent** you will be good at a skill without realising it, as your confidence grows you naturally become better and better and before long you will be completely confident in job interviews, just as the baby learning to walk, will one day walk without thinking about walking and balancing.

Now you have to become unconsciously competent at job interviews, don't just read this book practice, practice and practice. Do the research and ask others to question you, take each technique and practice them on family and friends, with Employment King's careers advisors and in mock interviews, as repetition is the key to learning any skill. To truly become unconsciously competent at influencing interview, <u>use live interviews</u> as mock interviews...

Rule No.45 Conceal Your True Purpose in a Mock Interview

"To find what you seek in the road of life, the best proverb of all is that which says:"Leave no stone unturned"
- Edward Bulwer Lytton

Completing mock interviews with Employment King's careers advisors will really help you master the skills we are teaching in this book and I would add that nothing beats a real life interview.

I recommend applying for any job that you don't want but you know you will be able to secure an interview for; this is often a job a salary below your current career salary. This way you can experience the nervousness that accompany job interviews and hopefully you will be asked enquiring questions that will put you on the spot.

As we all know practice makes perfect, this experience in a "safe" job interview (a job interview for a job you don't want) will help get you used to the interview experience and process, allowing you to put your new interview influencing expertise into practice. And what is good, you can make mistakes as you are not here to receive a job offer you here to master your interview skills.

As you make a mistake, take a mental note and then use this feedback to improve your interview skills for your next job interview - the position you really want. One mistake most people make without correcting it, is not creating a sellers persuasion loop, embedding your unique selling points through the interview.....

Rule No.46 Create a Persuasion Loop

"Knowing is not enough; we must apply. Willing is not enough; we must do" - Johann Wolfgang von Goethe

At the end of each job interview, you will have your chance to ask questions to the interviewer and when you download the free e-book **Tricky questions, killer answers** you will be given a list of possible questions you could ask. But one trick most people miss is it not to take this opportunity to summarise how you can add value, creating a persuasive loop from the interview start to the end, embedding your unique selling points throughout the whole interview.

Throughout the interview, when asked a question you will end each interview answer with a summary relating back to the original question, highlighting one of your unique selling points, creating a mini loop from the opening of the answer (answering the question in the first line) to the question end (the summary)

At the interview end when you're requested to ask the interviewer any questions, ask a few planned questions and then end the meeting by summing up the whole interview. Use this point to **emphasize your unique selling points**, creating a persuasive loop from the interview beginning (tell me about yourself - question) to the interview end (do you have any question for me - question)

Summaries in a way that seems to the interviewer that you have just decided to say this rather than the interviewer knowing you have planned a summary. You can see examples throughout this book where I have referred to earlier techniques, in later chapters to reinforce the importance of several Rules of Influence.

In your end of interview summary you need to:

1. **Highlight your selling points**
2. **Show your enthusiasm**
3. **Confirm how well you would fit in with the job/working for their company**

You need to summarise after you have asked the interviewer several job related questions and to make this statement sound like it is unplanned "off the cuff"

Example

"I just like to say, I'm really excited about everything you have told me about the company, I know my experience will fit in well with your company and I am already thinking of several ideas that will help us sell x"

As well as impressing the interviewer with your structured and detailed interview answers and industry expertise, you can learn how to energise the interview through a dynamic presentation....

Rule No.47 Interactive and Energetic Presentations Create Intrigue

"The world is but a canvas to our imaginations" - Henry Thoreau

I wasn't planning on writing a section on presentations, as this book is about becoming confident through using persuasion techniques to win job offers, but so many people e-mail me about delivering powerful presentations, I thought I would add this section for free.

6 Steps to winning Presentations

1. **Plan Your Story** a great presentation will flow like a story; you will need a beginning (Introduction), middle (Content) and end (Conclusion).
2. **Grab the Attention of the Audience** start with an exciting opening question "Did you know x?..." "Have you heard about this exciting x?.." or an engaging story "I want to share with you a little secret.." or "I have doubled the company profit in the last 3 organisations I have worked for and today I share my knowledge with you..."
3. **Keep the Audience Engaged** move around the stage/platform, use hand gestures, images, props (depending on your audience) ask questions, use facts, quotes and percentages. I like to get the audience involved, but again you need to decide if this is relevant to your job interview.
4. **Use Nested Loops** many people are addicted to TV soups, this is because they use nested loops, they start one exciting story and add a second story line along the way, and this is to keep the audience engaged. Start your presentation discussing point A , half way through start a second relevant point (B). Finish story B and return to point A.
5. **Use confidence Techniques** for any type of presentation or public speaking you need to act confident, by using the techniques described in an earlier chapter.

6. **Practice, Practice and Practice** like with all these techniques you need to practice and practice, you need to fully learn your content and be prepared to be asked questions on your presentation, this way you can get your key points across to the audience several times throughout the presentation.

With the basics of interview influence under your belt, you have prepared and researched the job interview, but it goes without saying, the interview starts when you arrive, but its how you influence when you arrive that really counts....

Interview Questions and Presentations

1. Use industry forums to gain sample industry interview questions
2. Research the company website to get an insight into the company values
3. Structure your interview answers so it meets the criteria of the interview question
4. When answering interview questions, start by answering the question in the first sentence, give detail and create intrigue and finally summarise the interview answer
5. Practice, practice and practice as repetition is the key to mastering answering interview questions
6. Complete real life mock interviews
7. Use the end section of the interview where you can ask questions to summarise your key selling points
8. Practice your presentations until you can deliver the presentation without prompts

---

Part Two

The Interview

Interview Arrival:

Influential Rules 48 to 51

The interview starts when you leave the house, as you walk to your car – you must walk confidently, as you choose the music you are going to listen to on the journey – you must pick confidence boosting music. You need to act successful from when you get up telling yourself that **"You can do it"** until you get home.

As you're walking towards the interview venue, there is a chance the interviewer may be watching, not purposely (we hope) but just by chance, which means your walk to the venue could be the interviewer's first impression of you which you know is highly important.

So it goes without saying that in the reception area when you introduce yourself and while you're waiting to be invited in to the interview you need to <u>act like the successful and confident person that you are,</u> as you never know who is going to walk past without you realising.

What is really important to remember is you have to act the way you want to come across from arriving at the interview until you leave. A company in America who recruited once a year wanted to recruit employees with excellent people skills, to decrease the amount of customer service complaints they were receiving as an overall business. The company had found out that the high number of complaints, were about just a few members of staff, which was the reason why they wanted a thorough recruitment process designed to detect potential candidates with potential bad customer service skills. They used a simple system, they had 100 candidates to interview, and they asked each candidate to give a 5 minute presentation about themselves in front of the other 99 candidates and asked the other candidates to listen to each presentation. The company placed their recruitment staff around the room, making notes. Their focus was not on the presenters, they were in fact observing the audience, checking which candidates were texting on their phone or talking during the presentations, if you were spotted you were rejected as an applicant.

Rule No.48 Get Others to Do The Hard Work – Get the Receptionist To Sell you to the Boss

"It is not enough to have a good mind, the main thing is to use it well" - Rene Descartes

Take control from the beginning, while most people go to an interview, give their name to the receptionist and sit down worrying about the coming interview, they are all missing a big opportunity – INSIDE INFORMATION!

When you give your name and sit down, make small talk with the receptionist **"How long have you worked here?"** **"Do you enjoy it here?"** and then ask **"What is the manager like?"** you will start to learn the mangers likes and dislikes; the receptionist might respond with **"The manger is great but you need to get your work in on time as she's a stickler for deadlines."**

As you can see you are getting valuable information, when you're asked questions in the interview, ensure you add your new information within your answers.

While making small talk ask the receptionist friendly questions, all you need to do here is ensure the receptionist likes you – if the receptionist is busy you will be best advised not to interrupt them or the feedback to the manger may be negative. As you have a friendly chat with the receptionist using the rapport building techniques, **the receptionist will compare** you with other interviewees who sit there quietly fidgeting with their head downs creating a more positive impression of you.

You may even get to the stage where the receptionist says something along the line off **"You seem really nice I'm sure you will do great in the interview.."** which you can reply with **"Thank you, you will have to tell your boss how nice I am it might help me get the job.."** this little joke may actually spur the receptionist on to telling the manger how nice you are.

With many companies the interviewer, between interviews will often discuss the interviewees with the receptionist and it can only help if the receptionist has several positive things to say about you reinforcing the interviewer's positive impression of you.

There is a chance that you may be up against other interviewees who the receptionist is also fond of, so one naughty technique is to turn the other interviewees into nervous wrecks....

Rule No.49 Turn Other Interviewees into Nervous Wrecks

"It is not the strongest of the species that survive, nor the most intelligent, but the one most responsive to change"- Charles Darwin

The first impression counts and as we said earlier, interviewers unconsciously compare interviewees and there is no better way to create a positive first impression is by having the interviewee before you act like a nervous wreck.

I have added this section more to highlight the power of using NLP and psychology in job interviews as I myself would not use this technique as I believe it is unfair – but you can do what you feel is right for you.

The mind focuses on what you are thinking, when you use the confidence technique in previous chapters, you are directing your mind to think about you acting confidently in a job interview, as the subconscious mind does not know what is real or not, which means the confident pictures you create are stored as memoires, the more you re-play this confident movie in your head the more instilled it will become until very quickly your mind believes you are a confident person and will you start to act as a confident person.

To highlight the power of influencing people easily, try this exercise: read these words aloud – **bed, rest, awake, worn-out, snooze, bedspread, doze, slumber, snore, tired, dream, lethargic, peace,**

yawn, drowsy. Now close this book and write a list of the words you just read.

Don't worry about any words you missed, but let me check did you record the word sleep? Was it one of the first words you recorded? Look back at the list of words you read out, was sleep one of the words I asked you to record? No, because I have just influenced your mind.

You can use this same mind power with another interviewee making them feel like a nervous wreck before the interviewer invites them into the interview room.

1. **Create rapport with other interviewees by making small talk and introducing yourself**
2. **Ask "Are you starting to feel nervous?" they will in most cases reply with "Yes"**
3. **From this, start a conversation about interview nerves.."I hate feeling nervous before interviews, when your stomach feels that it's in knots..."**
4. **Ask questions about positive things to keep rapport going "Where have you worked before?" and then follow this up by getting the other interviewee to imagine a negative interview "I hope they don't start asking obscure questions that you can't answer.." Use all 3 sensing words; visual, kinaesthetic & auditory**
5. **Keep this going asking questions both positive and negative, the main point here is to focus the person's mind on a negative interview, because if he imagines a negative interview he will feel negative and I would add this tactic shouldn't be used unless you feel this is your last hope.**
6. **For this to work you have to keep rapport and sound like your nervous yourself which is the reason why you're talking about a negative interview**

By the end of a short conversation your competition will be feeling anxious and nervous which can be hard to come back from and more importantly the interviewer's first impression of him will be negative compared to the confident first impression you will give. You may have come across this before while in a theme park **"Don't think about the scary ride/the height of the ride/that you were sick on, last time"** this negative command, commands you to think about what a person is telling you not to think about.

With nervous competition, we can return the focus back on you and one of the most common errors during job interviews is forgetting the interviewer's name, leading to an embarrassing interview...

Rule No.50 Increase Likeness by Using Names

"Success is to be measured not so much by the position that one has reached in life as by the obstacles which he has overcome while trying to succeed" - Booker T. Washington

We can all remember faces far more easily then we can remember names, at the initial stages of the interview when you are introduce to the interviewer by name, this is when you are at your most nervousness which means, you're in the worst state to be remembering new names.

Using an interviewers name during your conversation can increase rapport, which means you need to learn how to remember the interviewers name in just 5 easy steps.

1. **First imagine <u>your type of person who can remember names</u>, imagine you can see yourself in your mind's eye remembering the names of the people you meet, imagine how it would feel if you could recall people's names when you needed to.**

2. **When introduced to someone look for any characteristics that stick out, a big nose, dimples, large eyes etc. In your mind, create an image of their face and exaggerate any characteristics as you would if you were drawing a cartoon**

make the nose really big so you can see the hairs hanging down from their massive nostrils.

3.   In your mind write their name underneath the exaggerated cartoon face you created.

4.   Repeat the name out loud "Michelle, was it?" ensure their name matches the name you recorded in your minds drawing

5.   As an extra step, think of someone you know with the same name and in your mind match any exaggerated features (they both have large eyes) or imagine the second person was stood behind them jumping up and down shouting "It's Michelle, it's Michelle" or imagine the second person waltzing around the first person – once you associate the two people you will easily remember their name.

The trick here is to make a visual association and attach a name to it, which means next time you meet this person or throughout the job interview when you need to recall their name you will first remember the attached association (the big nose or your friend dancing around them) which will then trigger the person's name either through the name appearing under the cartoon picture in your mind or because you can instantly remember your friends name who is jumping up and down behind them.

Practice this technique at the next party you go to by trying to remember as many people's names as you possibly can, because once you can remember names you can find out what the interviewer is really secretly looking for....

Rule No.51 Catch Big Fishes with Big Hooks

"Ask yourself what makes you come alive, and go do that, because what the world needs is people who have come alive"
- Howard Thurman

As you shake hands and introduce yourself to the interviewer, you will often be asked an opening question such as **"Did you find us OK?"** or **"How was your journey?"** these are general questions designed to get you talking and to put you at ease before the real interview questions start.

As you answer, slip in your own question; **"Yes I found the building easy I came down yesterday so I knew I would be on time I hate to be late for anything."** (by highlighting that you are reliable – "You don't like to be late" you have started the process of building a positive impression of you from the interviewers point of view) as you sit down at the desk, ask **"Have you been interviewing all day?"**

After they have answered **"Yes"** you can follow this up with **"It must be hard trying to choose the right person** (you could add a sneaky point at yourself here, as we have added an embedded command – more on that later) **How do you know who to pick?"**

The interviewer may say **"I just have a gut feeling"** if you leave a gap (don't say anything) they might add, **"I can tell when someone is...*Essential Criteria*"** all you need to do now is repeat the essential criteria as part of one of your answers in the forthcoming interview questions **"One of my personal strengths is that I *Essential Criteria*"**

So, basically all you do is **Ask, Listen and Repeat** – easy; use what you hear as your bait, to hook the employer.

Remember you need to be confident and have good rapport for this to work well and to go unnoticed.

The interviewer will often start the interview by discussing the company history, duties and benefits, here is a great chance to ask more questions and to listen out for the skills, qualities and essential criteria the employer requires and then use these criteria's when answering future interview questions. Ask:

- **"How long has the company been in operation?"**
- **"What is the company mission?"**
- **"What type of person are you looking for?"**
- **"Where do you see the company being in the next few years?"**

These questions have to be put to the interviewer in such a way that it seems like a conversation not a question and answer session. You have to listen to what the interviewer says especially to the question **"What type of person are you looking for?"** and use their replies to answer your questions.

I agree, it does sound easy doesn't it? And I would add it is easy if you take some time to practise asking questions as part of a conversation with friends and family. As you know practice makes perfect, pick a certain thing you want to learn about a friend (maybe their routine before going to work) and start a conversation asking questions to unpick the details; do they use the same routine everyday or prefer to have variety? Etc

Understanding the employer's criteria through reading the job specification, researching the company values or by just asking them will improve your chance of a job offer. To be an effective seller you have to sell the key selling points of the product that are relevant to the buyer. You need to know how to sell your strengths, you need to be thorough with your research and to understood the importance of meeting the employers criteria while answering technical interview questions, but the key to interview success is having a natural ability to build rapport....

Interview Arrival

1. Learn about the employer by questioning the receptionist
2. Make other interviewees nervous by focusing them on negative interview experiences
3. Make associations to easily remember interview names
4. Question the employer to enquire what criteria they require as essential – then repeat these criteria's as part of your interview answers

Rapport – The Key to Success:

Influential Rules 52 to 56

Have you ever walked into a bar, a restaurant or a party alone and for some reason there was that one person (male or female) who you thought, without knowing why, that you could talk to them and you would just easily get on? You probably quickly spotted the people that you knew would rub you up the wrong way too. It's the same when starting a new job, working out in the gym or even walking your dog in your local park, sometimes you meet people and you just know you will **click-** this is because we like people who are like us, your unconscious picks up on people's behaviour, posture, voice tone and many other elements and puts all the people in the party/gym/new workplace into groups, the over arching group is Nice or Nasty; Friend or Foe.

I knew two people who started at a car dealership at the same time, one – Paul, started their because he had a passion for cars and knew all the makes and models, all the pros and cons for each model, to be honest there wasn't much this guy didn't know about cars. The second man James applied for the position because he loved working with people, he was a chatty and charming man who enjoyed helping others and felt working at a dealership would give him some reward knowing he has helped a family buy a car that suited their needs. In the first week James and Paul undertook the dealership Sales training programme, where they learnt all the techniques and tricks of the trade to sell good quality cars to customers, they learnt basic communication and language patterns as well as learning the basics of the automobiles as a product.

Over the first 2 months, Paul sold two cars to every one car of James', the manager was impressed with both new sale assistants as they were both selling more cars than his typical new recruits, but especially with Paul who was outselling James 2-1. James was successful because he had a natural ability to put customers at ease, to find out what they wanted and to help them to choose a car that would suit them. Paul was successful because he knew everything about cars, if you wanted a car with high speed or great brakes Paul would know which car won which award; it was his passion and product knowledge that was selling him cars. Over the next several months Paul continued to sell cars at the same rate and James was slowly increasing his rate of sales. After a couple of months they were neck and neck on the sales league board, Paul still selling due to his knowledge and expertise and James due to his customer service skills and personality, as well as his increase knowledge in cars, as over the months he had built up his knowledge and expertise to the same level as Pauls, as James use to say **"If I know my product better I will be in a better place to help my customers"** after several more months James had jumped ahead in the sales targets selling 2 cars to everyone car of Paul's, by now they both had the knowledge and expertise to sell cars, explaining the technical aspects of the engine and features, but James had the additional and most important skill a sale person requires, he had excellent peoples skills. After several years James' original customers would come back to upgrade their car and due to James' personal approach his customers were asking for him by name.

Rule No.52 Gain the Interviewer's Agreement

"Though no one can go back and make a brand new start, anyone can start from now and make a brand new ending"
- Carl Bard

A great way to increase rapport is to nod (in a yes motion) while the interviewer is discussing a serious point, unconsciously he will process this as you being interested in what he has to say. (You can also add to this by slightly leaning forward)

You can also use nodding when you are answering a question with a killer selling line. As you're speaking nod your head slightly, as you are in rapport with the employer they will nod their head or agree with you internally without releasing that you have influence them.

Using your body and posture to influence the interview is a sneaky but excellent way to gain the upper hand, you can also using "finger pointing" to gain agreement. To do this, say a general line such as **"To increase portability you need someone who is determined and positive..."** As you say this point to yourself as you would do if you were pointing to yourself unconsciously which means your point would only last a few seconds, as you don't want the employer to feel you have pointed purposely. Remember we talk with words and gestures and our unconscious minds listens to our words and movements, by pointing to yourself while saying a key selling point you are saying to the interviewers unconscious mind **"I am determined and positive.."**

With an interview only being a short period of time you need to learn how to build rapport quickly and then infect the interview with your personality....

Rule No.53 Infect the Interview

"The ultimate measure of a man is not where he stands in moments of comfort and convenience, but where he stands at times of challenge and controversy" - Martin Luther King Jr.

Knowing how to gain instant rapport is a great skill to possess and an easy skill to learn, you can already think of a thousand situations when getting anyone to like you instantly would be useful.

Today you will have a better understanding of how to create rapport with a Stranger or Interviewer instantly and how to use this to your advantage.

Rapport creates trust, helping us achieve our goal; getting a discount in a shop to passing a job interview. In NLP Rapport is defined as the establishment of trust, harmony and co-operation in a relationship.

How to Build Rapport

- We like people who seem familiar to us, who appear as we do. One way to increase rapport is to match the other persons Posture
- While in conversation, match how the other person stands or sits (creating a mirror effect) and copy their common gestures
- Listen to the person's language and match their voice speed and tone, which means you can even match and build rapport over the phone during a telephone interview
- Also, listen to the words the person uses, do they use **Visual, Auditory or Kinaesthetic language?** Match the interviewers language to gain rapport and to influence

The Power of a Smile

If you entered a room with two people stood there, you had to choose one person to talk to, they both looked the same, had a similar posture, and the only difference was one was smiling – who would you prefer to talk to?

- Everyone is attracted more to someone who smiles, as a smile shows warmth, confidence, happiness and acceptance. During an interview, where we all know first impressions count, if you walk into the room confidently with a big wide smile you will instantly be liked.

Listen

We have all hear the old saying **"We have two ears and one mouth, we should listen twice as much as we talk"** this is very true especially during job interviews

- Start a conversation by asking a question, as the other person talks keep listening and nod throughout the conversation. This will increase Rapport especially when you match their body language
- Listening builds rapport, by listening instead of interrupting with your own thoughts; it shows the other person the conversation is <u>about them not you.</u>

Future Pace

- After listening to the other person, build up and expand on what they have said, showing you have further knowledge and expertise. If possible add an idea/suggestion they have not thought of
- As an example, many interviewers will tell you about a new contract they have won (the reason they are recruiting – as an example: building FLT engines), as you sit there, smile, nod and listen, building up rapport. As the interviewer finishes, tell them how great it is to hear that they have won a contract in these competitive times, and how **(add in a further knowledge)** *the company could also use the engineers to delivery on site maintenance and breakdown repairs, as this would not increase overheads and pays well.*
- It doesn't matter if the company will take on this idea, it shows you have knowledge in their sector and can think out of the box, plus your first goal was to establish excellent rapport which you have easily done

Building rapport is easy, mirror the interviewer's body language, smile, listen to what they have to say and share your recently built up expertise, what is even more interesting is that rapport is a kind of "pacing" and once you can pace someone you can influence them through "leading" the interviewers thoughts....

Rule No.54 Take the Interviewer on a Journey of Discovery

"Don't judge each day by the harvest you reap, but by the seeds you plant" - Robert Louis Stevenson

Imagine attending a job interview and for some reason you get a feeling the employer is not fully convinced you are the right person for the job, how does this make you feel? As the nerves increase, your mind goes blank and you start to forget your carefully planned interview questions and answers.

To counter this, you need to change the direction of the interview and implant ideas into the interviewer's subconscious. This rule will allow you to **pace and lead** the interviewer, increasing rapport while taking the interviewer on a journey to discovery how valuable you really are.

Pacing and Leading

The pacing and leading technique has been around for a long time, often used in sales, for this technique to be effective, pace the interviewer's current situation, creating a **"Yes"** set, followed by a lead – your suggestion or command.

During an interview session, we would pace the interviewer, as a hypnotist would pace his client, by pacing their current experience;

Hypnotist **"As you are sat in the chair, listening to my voice...."** The client can only agree with this truism **"Yes I am sat in a chair, yes I am listening to your voice"**

As the client automatically agrees, add in your suggestion or command; Hypnotist **"You are starting to feel sleepy"** the client will carry on saying yes **"...Yes I am feeling sleepy"**

- Basically you Pace, Pace (pace again if you like) and then Lead.

Let's look at this in an interview situation, you can't say to an interviewer **"You are sitting down, listening to my voice, you want to give me the job."** or you can't for that matter, start to dangle a gold watch in front of their face, swinging it from side to side saying **"Give me the job, give me the job"** in these two situations you will probably be asked to quickly leave.

You can pace and lead any interviewer and I would add you need to pace and lead the interview without it being too obvious – pace and lead the conversation as part of your interview answers.

"You have recently won a new contract (Interviewer; "Yes") **and you want to ensure your team meet the contractual specifications,** (Interviewer; "Yes") **and from looking over my CV, you will <u>want to hire someone with my in-depth knowledge and experience to lead your team,</u> successfully achieving all the contractual targets** (interviewer; "Yes I can see you leading my team..I will offer you the job") **to achieve this goal I will XYZ"**

The interviewer won't be shouting out **"Yes"** but will be agreeing internally, imagining you **"Leading the team successful"**. This technique is about getting the interviewer to imagine what you want them to do, because if they visualise it, they feel more compelled to do it, this is due to people associating emotions to their visualisations.

"Your company has been established for over 34 years and you specialise in selling Egyptian Antiques abroad and in the UK, you are looking to <u>recruit someone like me</u> with a passion for history along with the skills and experiences to sell antiques"

Did you spot the pacing and leading?

"You have already said you are looking to employ a young and enthusiastic person with a creative mind who can handle responsibility, <u>give me the job</u> and I will use my creativity and enthusiasm to add value to your company."

Alone using just one pacing and leading statement will not gain you millions of job offers, you are trying to influence the employer thoughts and image of you throughout the job interview and when the employer imagines **"giving you the job"** **"recruiting someone like you"** or **"seeing you leading the team"** or any other embedded command you have told them to do, you are more likely to gain more job offers, aren't you?

As discussed in the earlier sales chapters, to win interview offers you need to consider both your influencing skills and the competition. Every superhero has a weakness, find the competitions kryptonite and destroy them...

Rule No.55 Interrogate the Competition

"He who asks is a fool for five minutes, but he who does not ask remains a fool forever" - Chinese Proverb

When managing a sports team the manger is interested in two elements, how he can get the best out of his team and how the other team perform – their strengths and weaknesses. A business person looking to break into a new market will compare their product to the product of the competition, to ensure they have the upper hand.

Understanding the competition can be crucial especially in group interviews and when applying for internal vacancies. With internal vacancies you may already know your competition, if you work with them on a daily basis. If the opponent's are from a different department you may know someone who knows them, which means you need question these resources.

All you need to do first is make a list of the person(s) strengths and weaknesses

Candidates Name	Candidates Strengths	Candidates Weaknesses

Now you have a list of the competition's strengths and weaknesses, add your name to the list and look at what your positives and area of developments are.

First, by weighing up the competition in this way, you now have a list of the competitions weaknesses and from a motivational point of view, it feels good to look at the competitions negative points, especially if their weakness is your strength.

Secondly, with a list of your own weaknesses, you can now think about preparing your interview answers to possible questions such as **"What are your weaknesses?"** – use the tricky questions, killer answers e-book to support you with this.

Knowing the competition's strengths means you can look at the job specification criteria and match their strengths to the criteria, if Joanne is good at X and the criteria requires Y then you having nothing to worry about as Joan will spend the whole interview talking about X while the interview will be thinking **"Who cares I need someone with Y."**

In many cases you will find that your competition has strengths that are required by the employer, which means you know what the other person's selling point will be. In this situation you have two options; you can use both or pick your preferred method.

1. **Negative Reinforcement** say Joanne did well in project X and this will be her main selling point. In certain situations throughout the interview (but not too many) you can add a negative slant on the project – this has to done in a general way so as not to make clear that you are putting another candidate down. Interviewer **"what are your strengths?"** Interviewee **"My key strength is time management, as an example if I was in charge of project X I would of X, Y and Z this would have increased efficiency saving X% of time in man-hours, giving the company an overall saving over £XXXX's..."** this allows you to highlight your strengths while putting down the other persons key selling point – why didn't they do X, Y and Z?

Don't keep referring back to one project though as this will become suspicious, the trick here is to highlight only your strengths and let the employer reframe your answer as a negative of your competition.

Another example, let's say Joanne's selling point is her **empathy/people skills** you can use the same technique to sell your strengths and to weaken her selling point. Interviewer **"Why should we offer you the position?"**

"The key to making this project a success is down to the amount of businesses that sign up to the scheme, on the face of it, it sounds like the project requires a manager with people skills and empathy but in reality we need to recruit a person with both people skills for when the project is in motion and someone with good business sense and sales skills to network and to gain more referrals. My experience in sales...."

Again you have sold your strengths while using the other person's selling point as a weakness without making it sound as if you're out to get a certain person, and without you sounding like a negative employee.

2. **Highlight Your Own Success** if you have worked on a project that the other person will use as their selling point, you can at some point in the interview explain how you made the project a success, not by taking all the credit unless this is valid but by talking about a particular point that you completed. Remember people generalise, when Joanne says how she led a successful project that met the targets etc, the interviewer will just generalise that she did all the hard work, what you are doing is showing how you were an integral part of the team.

    If you have a required skill or quality that Joanne has, you need to prepare your interview answer well, as you already know what type of answer Joanne will be giving, so spend time planning and rehearsing answers to highlight the key skills that both you and other candidates possess.

During one to one interviews, the spot light is on you which is great as this gives you a great opportunity to highlight your skills and to sell your strengths using all the techniques you are learning throughout this book, but in a group interview the situation is completely different as you have to fight for the spotlight and get noticed...

Rule No.56 Create an Aura of Power

"Happiness is when what you think, what you say, and what you do are in harmony" - Mahatma Gandhi

Interviewers use a variety of methods to interview job hunters, the most common is a one to one interview closely followed by group interviews often used for sectors working within the public sector or a company that values teamwork.

Generally, when you gain a group interview you will be asked to complete a **group exercise** – build a bridge out of straws, complete a brain teaser or make a jigsaw, etc. The employer has no concerns if you complete the task or not, they are more interested in your reactions to others, your communication skills and how you work within a team.

1. Start by introducing yourself to the other interviewees and interviewers. Be polite and friendly and remembers people's names.

2. Listen to the instructions for the group exercise, if possible write them down.

3. The first thing the interviewer will look for is to see who joins in with the activities; group interviews are generally used by employers looking for team members. If you don't join in with the interview team activity, you probably won't work well within a team environment.

4. Join in with the group discussions and don't dominate, let others have their say and give your own opinion.

5. Boost group morale, by telling people when they have had a good idea or suggestion, if someone is being quiet, ask for their opinion. This will show the interviewers that you try to involve others and will suggest you have managerial skills.

6. Learn to compromise and accept others' ideas with an open mind, remember the idea of the task is to see if you work well within a team not to solve the problem – even though solving the problem can only help.

7. When someone disagrees with you, say "It's good to get everyone's opinions and ideas" and ask how the solution can be improved. Don't make disagreements personal, keep focused on the problem/solution, and remember you're a Team Player.

8. Prepare a list of questions you can ask the group to get them motivated "Has anyone come across this group exercise before?"

9. During the group feedback to the interviewer, demonstrate to the employer that you have participated in the group exercise and that you gave some of the input. Gain bonus points by being the group member who feedbacks (have other group members join in with you)

10. Be enthusiastic throughout and when asked questions by the interviewer, mention your experiences and how this helped you complete the exercise. If you knew the answer to the group task don't let on, slowly give hints to the group to pass the task. It's more important to demonstrate team skills rather than being someone who knows the answer immediately.

To win more job offers you need to demonstrate to the employer in all types of interviews, that you are the best candidate for this role. You want the employer to see you as a highly valuable prize and that without you they – the organisation, has lost out. You want your talent to shine through and I agree this is easier said than done which is why persuasive and hypnotic language is so powerful. If a hypnotist can get a sane man to dance around a stage like a chicken, then surely you can learn to gain agreement from interviewers, to command employers to do as you say, and to change the direction of the interview to where you want it to go. All it takes is for you to learn several of the following powerful persuasion and hypnotic language patterns...

Rapport – the key to success

1. Nod, to gain agreement
2. Mirror the interviewer's body and verbal language to increase rapport
3. Pace the interviewer using "yes sets" and follow this with an embedded command
4. Make a list of other candidate's strengths and weaknesses, to understand your competition
5. Encourage participation in group tasks and volunteer to feedback on behalf of the group

Persuasive and Hypnotic Language Patterns:

Influential Rules 57 to 67

I have been told on several occasions that I write e-mails as if I'm having a conversation with someone, which I think is a good thing as I often write e-mails when I want to talk to someone who isn't with me.

We speak differently then we write, in most books but not this one (and I will explain why, later on), each sentence and paragraph is grammatically correct but in conversations our language can be vague and influential because when we are in rapport we talk without thinking about our language and as interviews are conversations you can use persuasive language that will bypass the interviewers conscious mind, moving the listeners mind to a higher level of thought.

As you learn persuasive and hypnotic language patterns you can re-read this book and notice how many times I have slipped them into the paragraphs I have written, as an example of how easy it is to use these techniques.

The more you read this book the more you will understand how the language you use in job interviews affect the job interview outcome. When we listen to people we take their words and turn them into pictures as an example **"Don't think of a pink elephant playing football"** have you visualised a pink elephant playing football? You have, because we understand what people are saying by making visual representations of the words we hear. Depending on the image we create in our mind alters how we feel emotionally. You may be talking to two people at the same time discussing a forthcoming parachute jump, one person seems excited as he visualises the parachute jump as fun and adventurous, while the other person looks white and nervous as they visualise the parachute jump as a dangerous and frightening activity.

By knowing how to use hypnotic patterns to influence people can really help you change the outcome to your next job interview, as people can be motivated and influence by what you say and how you say it.

Rule No.57 Motivate With Pain, Motivate With Pleasure

"The tragedy of life doesn't lie in not reaching your goal. The tragedy lies in having no goal to reach" - Benjamin Mays

First, why do you want to pass your next job interview? Why are you looking for a new career? And why do you want to leave your current job? Write a list of all your answers:

We are each motivated by either **towards** or **away from** motivation; **pleasure** or **pain, the carrot or the stick**! We either move towards pleasure or get away from pain. A person who has decided to go on a diet maybe motivated by **wanting to be thin and healthy** - Towards or **to stop being fat and unhealthy** - Away From.

People motivated by these two traits can be recognised by the language they use in everyday conversations.

Towards Motivational Language

- Attain
- Gain
- Achieve
- Get
- Include
- Towards
- Can't wait to get there
- Accomplish
- Reward
- End Result

- Goals

Away – From Motivational Language

- Avoid
- Exclude
- Recognize
- Problem
- Don't like...
- Trouble Shooting
- Fix
- Steer Clear of
- Prevent
- Solve
- Fix
- Prohibit

Re-read your answer to the original question, "Why do you want a new career?" and check the language (towards or away from) you have used the most in your answer.

By listening to a person's language you can hear what it was is going on internally which means you can understand what motivates or stresses someone. Towards and Away-from language is highly powerful by listening to words the person is using you can alter your language to match theirs, speaking as a 'towards' person or an 'away-from' person, which will increase rapport and ensure your interview answers are fully understood.

An interviewer may say "We need to **avoid** the **problems** we had last year by hiring a manger that will **fix** these **issues**..." **Away From Interviewer**

A second interviewer may say "We need to **move forward** and **achieve** our **future goals**, by hiring a manger that can get the **end result** we desire." **Towards Interviewer**

You need to talk using the interviewer's motivational language preference, by answering the questions with Away From or Towards language patterns.

"Hire me and I will <u>solve the issues</u> you have been having"
"Hire me and I will <u>build you</u> a new more profitable company"

As you learn new language patterns, you will learn how to influence people, in time you will be able to link influencing language patterns together making your persuasive conversations even more powerful...

Rule No.58 When You Don't Agree with the Employer's Point of View Change the Direction of the Conversation

"The best way to have a good idea is to have lots of ideas"
- Linus Pauling

You will already use **linking words** everyday because they come out naturally in conversation all the time but our unconscious mind deletes them, allowing your conscious mind to concentrate on the point of the conversation, which means we can influence the interview by using **linking words** to move the interview in the direction we want it to go. The linking words will connect a statement you have paced from the employer to a statement that leads the employer to a new direction.

In an interview you will you want to move the conversation on, when an interview is saying negative statements **"I don't think you're ready for this promotion"** you can now link this negative statement to a positive statement, and the good thing here is most people concentrate on the last thing you say – **the positive bit! "You don't think I'm ready for this promotion, but you will feel different when I explain how I can exceed your targets"**

Linking Words

- Because
- Then
- But
- And
- Yet

But is a great linking word and links a negative statement to a positive statement or vice versa by making the interviewer delete the first statement. **"You're a great person but.."** when you hear this as an example after a recent date, you delete **"You're a great person.."** and concentrate on the line after **"But.."** In a promotional job interview the interviewer may say **"You didn't meet the targets on project x"** you can reply with **"The targets weren't met on project X but...**insert a great selling point **I was in charge of marketing and the website I designed won an award.."**

And is the most common linking word and I would add that **and** is a great linking word to use in interviews and that means you can add extra selling points to the end of any interview answer. **"The targets weren't met on project X but I was in charge of marketing <u>and</u> the website I designed won an award <u>and</u> I would add the website was the key element in incoming referrals."**

Yet can be used to move the conversation into a new direction without the interviewer realising what you are doing, they will just feel compelled to listen. You may not understand the theory behind this technique **yet**, but you soon will. Job interview example **"I can't see that working for us"** **"You can't see that working for you yet, but you will do when I explain how I achieved these results."**

Because works similar to the "and" linking word because both words link two statements while staying in the flow of the conversation, because the word **because** creates intrigue – what will he say next? **"I don't think I get what you mean"** **"You don't get what I mean <u>because</u> I haven't explained the evidence that back up these results"**

Then can help to lead the employer to a new direction **"I'm not fully convinced" "when I show you the results I have achieved <u>then</u> you will be fully convinced"**

We use linking words to move the employers thinking to where we want it to be, by using BUT to delete the first negative statements and the words AND, THEN, BECOUSE give you the ability to move the conversation on and the word YET and BECOUSE can create intrigue...with the employer asking themselves **"when will I know?"**

During the interview you will be using your new found skills to gain the interviewers compliance, before manipulating them to offer you the job, this next language pattern is design to get the employer to comply with everything you say....

Rule No.59 Gain Compliance By Getting the Employer to Agree With Everything You Say

"Life isn't about finding yourself. Life is about creating yourself" - George Bernard Shaw

Imagine being in an interview and the interviewer starts saying negative generalisations about you **"so you worked at X company, everyone I have met from there are always lazy workers.."** It is true, this is an extreme example but I would add this type of generalisation occurs all the time which means you need to know how to use persuasive language to change the employer's mind.

I appreciate that employers can use negativity during the job interview which means you will need to learn how to get the employer to agree with you and your ideas. Flexibility allows effective communication, by not disagreeing with the interviewer avoids resistance allowing you to influence on a higher level and with little resistance you can gain agreement.

Any of these opening lines will help you get out of all sorts of tricky interview situations, helping you change the employer's opinion about you.

"Yes I know, which means ...."
"I agree and I would add..."
"That is true, but..."
"I can validate this because..."
"I appreciate this, and...

By first agreeing, the employer will let their guard down as they probably expected a different or more confrontational response. With the guard down they are now ready to listen to your next suggestion through 'linking' **"...which means...and....becouse..."** gaining their compliance.

If you disagree with the interviewer, you may cause a rift which can be hard to overcome, which means using a technique to gain agreement will allow you to further influence the interview, taking a negative disagreement and turning it into a positive agreement.

"I can confirm there are lazy people working at X, which means I'm a hard worker as I wanted to leave X to find a company like yours with good work ethics."

What we are doing here is softening the person's belief or generalisation and because you agreed with them they are likely to agree with you.

Everybody's interview fears stem from the thought that the interviewer will uncover their weakness, take an instant dislike to them or generally have a negative attitude towards them, for interview influencers this isn't an issue, it's a challenge you will win by employing Rule 60 – changing the interviewer's opinion of you....

Rule No.60 Only Change the Employer's Opinion if the Employer Has Negative Thoughts Towards You

"The significant problems we face cannot be solved at the same level of thinking we were at when we created them"
- Albert Einstein

Imagine you are attending a job interview and for some reason you get a feeling the employer is not fully convinced you are the right person for the job, how does this make you feel? Don't be concerned about the negative gut feeling you feel, concern yourself with how you can influence the interview using any of the 73 rules of influence which is best suited for changing the employers opinion about you.

A conversational reframe or *Redefine* (Sleight of mouth pattern by Robert Dilts) allows you to influence a person's belief. A working example of this is when your manger says **"Your Late!"** you can redefine this belief by saying **"I'm not late (negative) I was delayed in traffic (positive)"**

The predicament with negative interviews isn't about which answers you messed up or if the employer initially likes you, it's about using every opportunity as a new selling point, because when you answer interview questions you need to meet one of the employer's essential criteria. You can't just show how you match their criteria it's about showing how you will add value to their team.

In NLP we use 'Complex Equivalence' to suggest one thing is related or means something else. We use the same process in the job interview but instead of saying **"*this* means *that*"** we will say the opposite **"it's not *that* (negative) it's *this* (positive)"**.

- **"Don't talk about the *negative* lets discuss the *positive*..."**

We have all been in interviews or meetings when the interviewer, will offer out their problems **"We didn't meet last month's targets"** these negative statements often leave to a negative discussion, and we all know that a negative discussion in a job interview will leave a negative impression about you through the law of association, which means you need to learn how to quickly change the direction of the conversation, through the persuasive line – it's not negative, it's positive. **"Last month's targets were unmet** (Negative), **but it's about what we can do to meet this month targets that counts, my idea is...** (Positive)**"** the conversation will now be on how to achieve this month's targets and not last months under met targets.

In a job interview situation an employer, for example may say **"Aren't you too old for this type of work?"** you can reply by changing the direction of the conversation from age to your work ethic **"My age isn't a concern, what you need to ask is how much work I can do and in my last position I was nominated 'Worker of the month' on three separate occasions, beating people half my age"**

Throughout this book an ongoing message is to gain interview compliance, turning your interviewer into a "yes" man. This next technique is a great example of how a short sentence can have so much power....

Rule No.61 Turn the Interviewer into a 'Yes' Man

"If your actions inspire others to dream more, learn more, do more, you are a leader" - John Quincy Adams

A great and easy technique to learn, that I have used throughout this book is adding a 'tag' question to the end of statements. A 'tag' questions increase interview compliance, getting the interviewer to say **yes** to you.

You will be able to increase interview compliance by adding a **"tag question"** at the end of a statement or question

"Does it not?"
"Don't you agree?"
"Can't you?"
"Isn't it?"

"Aren't you?"

"You really want to give me the job, don't you?" As you read this example, it may seem a little extreme but I would add you will have opportunities to use persuasive language patterns throughout the interview which means the more you learn how to use these language patterns naturally by practising on friends and family the easier it will be to sneak them in during the interview, don't you agree?

What you are doing here is unconsciously gaining the employer's agreement with any of your suggestions, aren't you? By displacing resistance at the end of each sentence and command. You will agree this language pattern is an easy way to gain agreement, isn't it?

Re-read some of the chapters and notice how many tag questions and the other various persuasion and hypnotic language patterns I have used to help instil interview confidence into your subconscious, I already know you have spotted a few of them, haven't you?

Rome wasn't built in a day. To influence the interview, you have to build upon each persuasive layer until you have a strong foundation. With a strong foundation you will be ready to truly manipulate – demanding a job offer...

Rule No.62 Demand The Employer To Give You The Job

"Words are a form of action, capable of influencing change"
- Ingrid Bengis

So, if we're learning hypnotic persuasion why don't we just command the employer to offer you a job? OK let's do it - first I need to test if this system works, clear your mind, take a deep breath in and don't notice the rate and pace of your eyelids as they unconsciously open and close and blink. Are you now aware of your eyelids movements?

You are, as I embedded a command **"Notice the rate and pace of your eyelids"** which made you aware of them, even though you have been blinking throughout reading this book, but you were unaware of this on a conscious level. We see embedded commands everywhere from **"Buy Me Now"** on advertisements to hypnotherapist telling a client **"You are feeling sleepy"**

To create an embedded command in an interview, you first need to set up the embedded command; the set up is sometimes referred to, as a weasel phrases in the world of NLP seduction (Ross Jefferies): Example:

"When you.."
"You can…"
"The more you…"
"You want to.."
"If you were to…"

There are hundreds to choose from, when you can come up with other ideas, write them down. Second, you need to add the "Command." Example:

"Feel…."
"Think about…"
"Imagine…"
"Notice…"
"Remember.."

Remember you can think of many more command words, command words get people to take action. To finish of the embedded command, you need to end the sentence with a State, Process or Experience (SPE's): Example:

"A change of mind"
"Excitement"
"That I am right"
"You agree"
"Joy"

"Offer me a job"

As you are already aware there are many SPE's you can use, we have just used a few examples to help you understand how embedded commands work, but with a little thought you will be able to come up with many more.

I'm in agreement, as you read the breakdown of this technique not all of it will make sense, but it's not about if the breakdown makes sense yet, it's about how you can learn to put it all together. As you read these next examples you will <u>start to understand embedded commands better than before</u>.

"When you feel excited about what I can bring to the organisation..." – <u>Feel excited</u> is the command

"If you want me to, I can explain the proposal in more detail...." – <u>You want me</u> is the embedded command

"The more you think about how you can offer me the job the more you will notice what added value I can offer" – <u>Offer me the job</u> and <u>notice what added value I can offer</u> are both embedded commands.

For embedded commands to be effective you first need to gain excellent rapport and the embedded command has to go unnoticed by others, for maximum effectiveness **change your tone of voice when giving the command** and leave a small gap before and after the command. For embedded commands to work talk slow, a good embedded command will bypass the conscious mind and head straight for the unconscious mind.

Many of you reading this book will be a parent or at the very lease you will have some babysitting experience, the next technique is used daily by parents to influence their children to take action, but most parents don't even realise that they are already master persuaders...

Rule No.63 Suggest to the Employer Not to Offer You the Job

"Take time to deliberate; but when the time for action arrives, stop thinking and go in" - Napoleon Bonaparte

Negative commands are a favourite of mine and are used by hundreds of parent's everyday without them even knowing it. When we tell a child **"Don't <u>eat those chocolate</u> biscuits while I'm out"** what happens? The child eats the biscuits.

The negative command **"Don't..."** sends a subliminal message to the brain giving an embedded command as the brain cannot process the negative weasel phrase **"don't..."** and only registers the positive statement **"...eat those chocolate biscuits while I'm out"**

Before we carry on, I don't want you to think about a beautiful beach, with golden sands and a deep blue sea! What did you just think about? A beautiful beach, right? This is the power behind negative commands.

You can use negative commands throughout a job interview and remember like with all hypnotic persuasion language patterns - you have to time the interview right before using them as these commands and suggestions work best when they go unnoticed.

Examples

- **"Don't <u>think about offering me the job</u> until I explain what else I can bring to the organisation"**
- **"I would recommend that you don't <u>make your mind up now</u> until I show you the evidence"**
- **"It's important that you don't <u>get excited</u> until I illustrate this highly profitable forecast"**

The job of the interviewer is to choose the best employee and we all like choice, having two options is better than one. I like to offer choice to the interviewer, especially when both choices lead them down the only path I want them to walk...

Rule No.64 Conceal Your Intentions by Simulating Choice

"The world needs dreamers and the world needs doers. But above all, the world needs dreamers who do"
- Sarah Ban Breathnach

Before we start, do you want to read the rest of this chapter now or later? Have you been given a choice here? You may think you have but you haven't as I have invited choice **"now or later"** but there is no choice as I have told you to read the rest of this chapter at some point (no choice) which was my objective. In NLP we call this illusion of choice a 'double bind'

- **"Would you like to offer me a job now or later"**
- **"I can summaries the proposal or explain it in full?"**
- **"Do you want me to start the presentation now or later?"**

To use the double bind technique, you need to be aware of your objective - what do you want to achieve; to highlight your personal skills, to discuss a previous successful project or to just be offered a job? From knowing your objective you can phrase a question offering two options that both end with your objective.

You may want to re-read this last part again; you can read it now or you can read it after the next chapter to let what I said seep in?

Your collection of persuasion techniques is growing, for many of you I recommend practicing these skills and re-reading previous chapters and techniques until you fully understand them. Once skilled in the art of persuasion you will be ready to master Rule 65 mind reading the interviewer...

Rule No.65 Make the Puppet Dance

"What you are is what you have been. What you'll be is what you do now" - Buddha

We have already talked about mind reading, but in this context – using NLP hypnotic and persuasive suggestions, we will claim to know the interviews thoughts and feelings by using unspecific sentences.

I know you are reading this book thinking about how you can use these techniques to gain more job offers which means you must be thinking about how well you can communicate in job interviews.

You can use **mind reading** to encourage the employer to think about what it is you want them to think about and it also can help to increase rapport.

- **"I know you are wondering how I can bring the same results I achieved from my current organisation to yours.."**
- **"You are thinking about increasing your targets..."**
- **"You may be curious about my marketing strategy..."**

Now you are aware of mind reading, watch commercials on TV and notice the amount of times marketers use mind reading **"I know you want to lose weight.."** **"You are thinking about your increasing debt.."** **"You want to go somewhere fun and hot for your next holiday.."** How to they know? Do I really want to go somewhere fun? When was I thinking about my increasing debt? Generalisations, like these often go unchallenged and unnoticed by most people, <u>including job interviewers</u>.

As you are learning, people are easily influence by your words. One of the key rules to influencing is the rule of social proof; people believe what others tell them, so in your next interview get others to sell you to the interviewer...

Rule No.66 Use Social Proof to Influence – get others to highlight your strengths

"Do not wait until the conditions are perfect to begin. Beginning makes the conditions perfect" - Alan Cohen

Using quotes and quoting percentages is a great way to highlight your strengths and hard work without having to sound to big-headed. You can add many of the above hypnotic suggestions to quotes, helping you influence the interview.

"I remember in my last company while working on a multi million pound project to build 3 new schools. I was looking at the project designs and my manger said to me "you know, I requested you for this project because I know that you get the job done on time to the high standards and I don't know how you do it, but you have a way of increasing the teams output by 15% which always increases our profit."

Quotes are powerful as we believe what other people tell us even if we don't know this person; this is the reason why books always record endorsements on the back cover or why companies pay millions to famous people to endorse their product.

A hypnotherapy friend of mind said **"hypnotic quotes are the best way to get someone to do something without them realising you are influencing them"**

Create intrigue and you will hook your audience, once hooked the interviewer will be feeding out of your hand and the best way to create intrigue is through story telling...

Rule No.67 Create a Fantasy

"Creativity is the ability to see and to respond"
- Erich Fromm

We have story telling routed in our past, from our ancestors passing down moral tales filled with metaphors designed to pass on learning to stories being told through TV and films. People use metaphors everyday as a tool to describe how they feel, you have heard common metaphors including **"I feel like a duck out of water" "I have the weight of the world on my shoulders" "You look as fresh as a daisy"** you will also notice that peoples body language and gestures match the metaphors they use.

I recently attended a consultation to help reduce the youth unemployment figure in Greater Manchester; the chair, a tall man determined to reduce the unemployment figure unconsciously used a metaphor to describe how he felt about tackling the situation **"To reduce the unemployment figure we need to <u>work as a unit</u> and <u>face our opponents</u>, by <u>striking from several fronts</u> we can <u>blast away any obstacle</u> and win this unemployment <u>battle</u>"** I thought to myself this is how it must have felt to be in Churchill's office.

When being interviewed by a person using a metaphor **"We are <u>branching</u> out", "We are looking for a <u>captain to steer our company</u> in a new direction" "It's like <u>flogging a dead horse</u>"** you can reply to their questions in a metaphorical way creating a <u>stronger bond</u> to <u>build a </u>better <u>relationship</u>. As an example when asked **"If you were recruited as our office manager how would you <u>build up </u>the team?", "To build up the team, <u>you first need good foundations</u> which means I will start by.."**

To practice replying to metaphors, record a reply to these 3 common metaphor interview questions

- **"How can you overcome this hurdle?"**
- **"We're looking for the right ingredient; do you think you will fit the bill?"**

- **"Can you handle the heat?"**

This section on hypnotic and persuasion interview techniques, has covered a vast amount of influencing patterns, it is like having a bag of ingredients with every ingredient being a different hypnotic language pattern. You can use the ingredients individually but when you put them together they create a stronger dish, and remember people pay hundreds of pounds for just one plate of something really special.

With all these persuasion and rapport building techniques under your belt, you have the knowledge and preparation to deliver winning job interviews...

Persuasive and Hypnotic Language Patterns

1. Motivate interviewers by wording sentences and interview answers with "towards" and "away from" language
2. Link negative statements to positive statements using "and" "because" & "but"
3. Agreeing with the employer softens their beliefs which allows to change the direction of the interview
4. Gain compliance by adding "tag" questions at the end of statements
5. Use embedded commands in the middle of sentences/interview answers
6. Use "don't" to negatively embed commands
7. Offer two choices that both lead to one objective
8. Give example quotes to highlight your strengths without having to sound big headed
9. Reply to the interviewers by responding in metaphor to their metaphor

---

Winning Job Interviews:

Influential Rules 68 to 73

A friend of mine, a runner always went the extra mile. He stuck to his intense training regime, ate healthy and completed all pre-race warm ups. What was different about my friend and other runners is that he would constantly watch videos of Olympic runners over and over again and he would read motivation books and books on healthy bodies. I understood the diets and training but I had to ask him why he read the books and watch videos over and over again. He told me that every little bit counts, as races are won on a 0.2 or 3% of a second, by learning to be at your best before a race by learning from the Olympic champions, by having a healthy mind and body you can increase your chances, sometimes by just 0.2 or 3% of a second but this 0.2 or 3% of a second could be the difference between a gold medal and forth place.

Rule No.68 An Argument Will Only Show Your Weakness

"If we did the things we are capable of, we would astound ourselves" - Thomas Alva Edison

During an interview delivered by a poor interviewer, you may be asked negative questions or you may just be put down by the interviewer, in this case I would be asking myself **"Do I want to work for a company like this?"** Often in cases like this you automatically respond defensively which is the wrong state for a winning interview, this 3 step plan will help you handle any stupid questions from stupid interviewers.

1. **Never get defensive.** If you get defensive at a negative question you will sound guilty **"You didn't meet your sales targets" "It wasn't my fault..."** this defensive answer, will only lead to a debate about their negative statement which is the one thing you want to avoid.

2. **Get Specific.** Many negative statements are generalised or distorted; you need to get specifics by asking the interviewer questions **"Which sales targets are those?" "Erm the one's from last week"** replies the interviewer **"Is that the sales target from XXX contract which I over achieved in or the sales targets from YYY contract that I gave advice on but wasn't involved with?"** Interviewer: **"Oh so you weren't really involved in the YYY contract.."**

As a second example, you may be told during a potential promotional interview **"the rumour is you're not been pulling your weight"** you may reply with **"Who exactly have you heard this rumour from?"** the interviewer can only answer by giving detail; **"Well Paul said you left the shop floor and sat in your office on Friday when we had that big job in."**

You have now taken a general statement and got the specifics from the interviewer, which allows you to reply positively. **"Friday, yes that was when you wanted the accounts report completing by,** would you have preferred the report completing or for me to tell help out loading the vans?"

3. **Change the Question Frame.** When asked a hard question or given a negative statement, you can reframe this question by offering a new positive question or statement. **"I don't think you have the imagination demanded for this particular performance"** this is quite a damaging statement, so you can respond with **"So, what you're saying is, if I have a creative idea for the show right now, you would be interested in hiring me, wouldn't you?"** by changing the **Frame** of the question, you will change the direction of the conversation, moving away from a negative situation or damaging statement, towards a positive conversation.

By handling negative interview questions positively, reframing them so the conversation moves to where you want it to be, will only help to create a more positive image of you. As well as handling potential damaging interview situations, you can turn the interview on itself and interview the interviewer....

Rule No.69 Turn Around the Tide of Power; Interview the Interviewer

"Life is like riding a bicycle. To keep your balance you must keep moving" - Albert Einstein

A good interview is more like a conversation compared to a set of interview questions and answers and once you are in a flow of a conversation, you will feel comfortable asking the interviewer your own questions, which means you don't have to wait until you're asked **"Do you have any questions for me?"** before you feel comfortable enough to question the interviewer.

Once you start asking your own questions your interview will **turn into a conversation** where you can interview the interviewer, which will give a more informed discussion when deciding whether or not to accept their job offer. And what would you prefer if you were an interviewer; would you prefer to ask another person the same old questions, and then wait for their response? Or would you prefer to have an interactive conversation where the answers to your questions have been discussed naturally?

These 4 tips will help you turn a standard interview into a positive conversation:

1. **Research.** First research the company and the job position, as often the position title can vary in duties depending on the organisation you work for. You need to make a list of what is important to the company, what skills, qualities and experiences the organisation requires. Even more importantly what are the company's' values, beliefs and the company mission? – This information is easy to locate through the company websites and especially for large organisations on online forums.

2. **Questions.** As you are asked questions, you can answer your interview question relating to your researched list of requirements – in essence you will be speaking the company language.

    You will start to see a lot of nodding as the employer agrees with your view point (as it will be the same view point the company takes) this will quickly lead to good rapport.

    Once in rapport, you can start to ask the interviewer questions, first on their requirements/values as this is something the company will feel passionate about and will answer freely.

    While asking the company requirement questions, slip in a question you would like to know the answer to **"What type of person are you looking to recruit?"** the interviewer will freely answer these questions.

3. **Having a Conversation.** By answering and asking relevant questions, the interview will naturally turn into a conversation,

often with the interviewer taking a second, to look back at the next question (which they forgot to ask due to the conversation) and then saying out loud something similar to **"OK, erm actually you have already answered this one.."** this unconsciously will re-enforce to the interviewer that you are the right person for the job.

4. **Job Offer.** Obviously with a large amount of rapport and the employer believing your values and work ethic are that of the organisation, you are likely to be offered a position. Unlike previous interviews where you answer a set of questions, selling yourself - this interview has been a conversation, where the interviewer has openly answered your questions - this has now given you a more detailed picture of the company (you will already have an overview from the research you undertook.) You now can make a more informed choice if you want to work for this particular organisation, as you will agree there is nothing worse than starting a new job and hating it within the first few weeks, I would also add using **this technique will secure you more job offers** giving you the option of organisations to work for – and this should be every job hunters main objective, to be able to pick a position from several job offers.

After a day of interviews, the interviewer needs to decide which person to offer a job to or who to take through to the next round of interviews. The problem here is the interview will often make this decision a day or two after the interviewer, which means you need to get the interviewer to remember your performance...

Rule No.70 Master the Art of Performance

"You can never cross the ocean unless you have the courage to lose sight of the shore." - Christopher Columbus

Think about 5 past good memories, why did you choose these 5 memories, out of all the hundreds and thousands of memories you could have chosen? Did you remember a birthday or Christmas when you felt excited? Was it a memory of a loved one; your first date or wedding day? Whatever memory you remembered, they all have one thing in common with my examples – you picked a memory with an emotional attachment as we remember emotional moments more easily.

This is why phobias are so powerful, the phobic person feels attached to this negative emotional memory which is why on the fast phobia removal technique we dissociated ourselves from the emotional memory. This means if you want to ensure the employer remembers you - **make a positive emotional attachment** during the job interview.

Throughout the interview you can use the sensing words which you learnt in an earlier chapter, these **visual, kinaesthetic** and **auditory** words will help you guide the employer to associate you with their company. To create a memorable association you need to put the employer into a trance like state, what we mean by a trance state is the state between sleep and awake, a day dream state – the same state that drivers have when on a long journey, when they realise their focus went from the driving to an internal focus, a memory or thought.

As a hypnotherapist I understand how easy it is to take people to that internal place of thought. A great word (or command) that will take people there is **"imagine"**

This word commands an internal focus and when used at the correct time during the job interview you can command the employer visualise you working in their organisation in a positive light, which will create a memorable interview performance.

"As you know I have a wide range of experiences, <u>imagine</u> I was working for you, I would get great results by..." when you say to the interviewer "imagine I was working for you" the employer has to imagine you working for them, and if the employer already likes you, they will imagine you working for them in a positive light. You can use the command 'imagine' to get the employer to visualise you in a range of employed situations.

"Imagine you wanted to recruit me..."
"Imagine me leading your team..."
"Imagine I doubled your sales figures, how would that make you feel?..."

A masterful performance will be remembered for a long time; encourage the employer to **imagine** you in the current role being successful, create intrigue and use stories to capture your audience's attention. Use the influencing techniques throughout this book to create a strong image of you in the future, meeting your targets, achieving new outcomes and adding value to the organisation.

By using all 3 senses **auditory, kinaesthetic and visual**, and the command **imagine**, you can create a strong emotional connection between you and the interviewer. Your goal here is for the interviewer to have that *gut feeling* about you, they need to feel *compelled to recruit you* and your influencing techniques need to be used to *create an unforgettable performance*.

With the interviewer blown away by your performance and the job offer on the tip of their tong, you are ready for that final push, the final incentive that will close the deal....

Rule No.71 Offer A Diamond With One Hand, Take It Away With The Other

"To a brave man, good and bad luck are like his left and right hand. He uses both." - St Catherine of Siena

The interview is broken down into several parts, from the introduction, followed by the interviewer's brief overview of the company, to the interviewer checking you are a suitable candidate, questioning you to extract what value you can add to the company, to the interview close.

Throughout the interview you will have used a variety of techniques to increase your chance of the interviewer realising you are the ideal person for this position. At the interview close stage <u>you need to close the deal</u>, to finally ensure the interviewer will choose you.

But, first you need to understand why people want what they can't have. **Scarcity makes us want a product more**, which is why collector's items are so valuable – there's not that many of them. I have a friend who collects album covers with faults; the guitarist jacket is the wrong colour, a name is spelt wrong. These items are worth quadruple the price of a normal collector's item even though the product was wrongly produced, the value is in the fact that this item is unique, one of a kind. And it's being one of a kind, a unique item that will secure you a job offer.

If you have followed the rules in this book, so have already sold your unique selling point and highlighted on several occasions the value you will bring to the organisation, so all that is left is to make yourself scarce.

If I was selling a necklace, I would put a big sign in my shop window saying **"Ruby Necklace Only 10 Remaining"** if I was selling an old comic I might say **"Limited Edition Superman Comic Only 100 Ever Produced"** but when making yourself look scarce at a job interview you need a different tack, but the psychology remains the same – the interviewer doesn't want to miss out.

With the interview being highly impressed with you, mainly due to your new selling skills or by you embedding commands in to your interview answers, telling him to recruit you, you next need to highlight that **you are not freely available** and you can do this in two ways:

- At some point towards the end of the interview, explain how you are under pressure from other companies to accept a job offer **"Thank you for inviting me to the interview today; I have really enjoyed meeting you and learning more about your organisation. I have a hard decision now, I'm really impressed with the vision you have for the company and I can see myself fitting in here really well, but a company that interviewed me last week is pushing for me to accept their job offer"** this is highly effective, especially when it sounds of the cuff and as if you really talking to yourself out loud.

- A different version is to use a similar line to highlight that you have 3-4 job interviews lined up. **"Thank you for today, I'm really impressed with your company I have several other interviews lined up this week for similar positions I hope they can match your high standards"**

Remember by this stage of the interview, the employer is already highly impressed with you, all you are doing here is saying, **"Look I'm not going to hold out for this job"** if you have done your homework and the interview has gone as planned, the interviewer will want to hire you anyway, but they can't as they have to follow their company policies and procedures and interview the other 4-5 candidates that made it through the first round of CV's and application forms, and now they have the fear that an opponent company may snatch you up first, making them want you even more.

By highlighting how you can add value to whichever organisation you accept a job offer from, the current interviewer or their competition, you are now taking the interviewer on an emotional journey. Taking them on a high when they realise how they can turn your skills into profit and down to a low when they realise that a competitive organisation is still in with a chance of recruiting you. This emotional journey will add to your unforgettable performance, but as we started on a high, you need to end on a high....

Rule No.72 End as You Started with Manipulation Mind

"When one door of happiness closes, another opens, but often we took so long at the closed door that we do not see the one that has been opened up for us" - Helen Keller

Towards the end of your great interview you will want to **finish on a high**, by this stage you will fully understand the employer's criteria; you will have suggested using hypnotic and persuasive language patterns that you are the only person they will think about recruiting and you will know what skills, qualities and experiences most impressed the employer.

As we do with our interview answers, you will need to summarise the whole interview – your unique selling points, at the end of the interview, only stressing the key points that most impressed the interviewer.

Towards the end of the interview, you will be asked **"Do you have any questions for me?"** have interview questions prepared (there are examples in the <u>Tricky Questions Killer Answers</u> e-book that you can download for free as part of buying this book). If you haven't prepared any questions or as you finish asking questions, you can reply with **"No, I think you have covered everything but I just wanted to say how impressed I am with you and how you described your companies work ethic/mission/goals** – whatever the company's key message is, praise goes along way when said sincerely, **and I know my** (add your criteria; skills, experience, etc – whatever most impressed the employer about you) **will work well within your organisation helping us to achieve the company goal."**

Remember the brain cannot remember every single detail, so what will the interviewer remember about you? You need to **ensure the interviewer remembers your key selling point**, as well as your characteristics that meet the employer's criteria – some organisations want a friendly and approachable person, while other companies will require someone who gets to the point quickly and can make demanding decisions.

By summing up the whole interview in one paragraph will allow the interviewer to store this last message that has been repeated throughout the interview, so when they think of you they think A, B and C – **your unique selling point**, that most impressed the interviewer throughout the interview.

As you have learnt throughout this book, practice makes perfect. When you re-read this book, you will notice many techniques and suggestions that you missed the first time round. It is the same in job interviews, the more job interviews you attend, the more proficient you interview skills will become. A quick and effective way to learn from past interviews is by looking at the interview from a different perspective...

Rule No.73 Look For Your Own Weakness and Stamp It Out

"Opportunity is missed by most people because it is dressed in overalls and looks like work." - Thomas A Edison

After every interview you need to evaluate your performance from different perspectives, helping you improve your interview techniques in preparation for your next job interview, as we said in **The Secrets of Employment E-book** you need to continue to job search until you receive a job interview in writing.

There is no failure only feedback, as you look at your interview in a different way you will take on new learning, using this new knowledge to better yourself as your goal is to have a choice of job offers to choose from.

Consider the Interview from your own perspective

Return to a passed interview fully in your minds eye and run a mental movie of this situation as it occurred on the day of your interview (It often helps to close your eyes). Re-experience this situation as fully as possible, (becoming totally associated with the emotions you had at the time of the interview) from your own eyes. What can you see? Notice the interviewer you are talking to, hear what they said to you. See the expression on their face, notice their body language. Become aware of how you feel. Speak to the person (out loud or in your head) and use the same language as you originally did. Really relive this experience as you did at the time of the interview. At the end of this episode, rewind this movie and pause the movie at the beginning of the interview.

Break your State by shaking your arms and legs!

The Interviewers Position

Now that your movie is 'paused' at the beginning, look over at the person interviewing you. Notice how the interviewer is breathing; notice their posture, facial expressions, the way they move. Now consider what their tone of voice is like, do they speak fast or slow, loud or quiet? How do they walk, talk, sit, laugh and relax? What are some of the things you know about this person; what are their likes and dislikes?

Now imagine floating out of your own body and into the body of the interviewer. Imagine you are inside the interviewer's skin. Become aware of how this person experiences life. Take on their posture, gestures and their tone of voice.

Set aside your own beliefs and values and replay the interview from the interviewer's viewpoint. Pay attention to the thoughts of the interviewer, their self talk and to any insights that surface as you observe the interviewee (you) in front of you.

Use the interviewer's language to describe what you experience (refer to yourself as you) ask the interviewee the interview questions asked at the time of the interview, look at how they respond and how they communicate to you the interviewer, what have you learnt from this viewpoint, what else can you learn the interviewers experience of the interview, how did the interviewee (you) come across?

After the scene ends, rewind and pause the video and float back into your own body taking with you this new learning and insights.

Break state again by shaking or taking 3 deep breaths.

The Interview Observer

Return to the interview from your own point of view, before you play out the interview for a third time, float out of your body and move to a detached place, where you can observe both you and the interviewer. Once again re-play the interview as if you were watching and listening to a film or live show. Be curious about what unfolds before you and notice the learning you gained from this third perspective. Listen to the conversation and notice the body language of both the interviewee and the interviewer and how you both interact and how you both respond to each other's communications.

After the scene ends, rewind the film and float back into your body bringing with you all the insights and learning from the three perceptual positions. Pay attention to the difference in your experience. Take all the time you need to fully return to yourself before opening your eyes.

Repeat this as many times as you feel is necessary and always end in the first position of you as the interviewee.

Ok, so what did you learn from this experience? _____
What went well for you? _____
What will you do differently at your next job
interview?_____

Winning Job Interviews

1. When asked negative questions, ask for specifics or reframe the interview question
2. Turn the interview into a two way conversation
3. Make emotional attachments with the interviewer
4. Make yourself sound scarce, as we all want what we can't have
5. Summarise your key selling points to the employer
6. Replay past interviews in your mind and view these experiences from different perspectives to increase your understanding and to improve your interview techniques

We have now come to the end of the book; you have built up a stack of resources that you can use, from understanding how to sell yourself to using persuasive language in the interview. Now you have a choice, you can use the techniques you have learnt, which means you first need to practice them to become unconsciously competent, as you need to sound genuine for these techniques to work or you can do nothing and hope for the best?

The key to winning job offers is making the employer fully aware of all the skills, qualities, knowledge and experience you posses. To do this you need to be an expert in your job role and industry as employers will recruit an expert over someone who doesn't really understand what their discussing. You need to be confident about what you have to offer - **your unique selling point** and know how to frame your answers to highlight yourself in the best possible light. And importantly you need to capture the employer's imagination and use their language to help them quickly process your interview answers, ensuring your message gets through. And I would add, as a bonus you now know how to use hypnotic persuasive language, body language and people's personality types to gain instant rapport, encouraging instant offers of employment.

Finally we would like to end by wishing you the best of luck with **Your Life, Your Career and Your Future.**

Chris Delaney
Employment King

www.employmentking.co.uk
www.christopher-delaney.com

E-mail info@employmentking.co.uk with any questions, queries and with all of your success stories.

Bibliography

Allan and Barbara Pease *(2004) The Definitive Book of Body Language*
Billy O'Connell (2005) *Solution-Focused Therapy*
Daniel Goleman (2006) *Social Intelligence*
David Hodgson (2006) *The Buzz*
David Keirsey (1998) *Please Understand Me 2*
David J. Lieberman (2000) *Get Anyone to do Anything*
Derren Brown (2007) *Tricks of the Mind*
Diana Beaver (1994) *NLP for Lazy Learning*
Elliot Aronson, Timothy D. Wilson, Robin M. Akert (2002) *Social Psychology*
Ian McDermott, Joseph O'Connor (1996) *NLP and Health*
Tom Stafford, Matt Webb (2004) *Mind Hacks*
Nicky Hayes (1994) *Understand Psychology*
Paul Ekman (2003) *Emotions Revealed*
Paul McKenna (2006) *Instant Confidence*
Richard Bandler (2008) *Trance-Formation*

- All the NLP techniques covered in this book, have been developed by techniques originally created by Richard Bandler and John Grinder taught to the author through a variety of NLP training courses

Robert B Cialdini (2009) *Influence*
Shelle Rose Charvet (1995) *Words that Change Minds*
Stan B. Walters (2000) *The Truth About Lying*
Steve Andreas, Charles Faulkner (1996) *The New Technology of Achievement*
William Poundstone (2010) *Priceless – the hidden psychology of value*

Also available by Employment King:
"The Secrets of Employment"
E-book, instant download, available by visiting
http://www.employmentking.co.uk/secrets.html

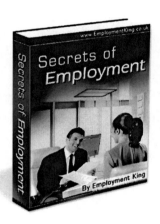

Business In Red Shoes. *"I wish this book had been available when I first set up in business. Unlike similar books Rebecca's book engaged me. It is practical and a doing book rather than talking at me. I would recommend this book not only to women thinking about going solo but also those who have already set up a business".*

Women In Business

Asymmetric Warfare for Entrepreneurs. *"I found this book to be an excellent read from start to finish. It has a mixture of sound business advice for the budding entrepreneur combined with very interesting excerpts from the classic piece of writing by TE Lawrence."*

www.mxpublishing.co.uk

CPSIA information can be obtained at www.ICGtesting.com
Printed in the USA
LVOW12s0624260714

396136LV00003B/151/P

9 781780 922225

table on so far...
tions to a fast-changing world has me...
ry much reflecting on my own over the past few years. A...
ted book which holds a mirror up to the world we live in."

Mark Beaumont

f adventure

Riding Out

RIDING OUT

Copyright © Simon Parker, 2022

An Hachette UK Company
www.hachette.co.uk

Summersdale Publishers Ltd
Part of Octopus Publishing Group Limited
Carmelite House
50 Victoria Embankment
LONDON
EC4Y 0DZ
UK

www.summersdale.com

Printed and bound by CPI Group (UK) Ltd, Croydon, CR0 4YY

ISBN: 978-1-80007-499-6

Substantial discounts on bulk quantities of Summersdale books are available to corporations, professional associations and other organisations. For details contact general enquiries: telephone: +44 (0) 1243 771107 or email: enquiries@summersdale.com.